Aloneness

to

Oneness

Todd Perelmuter

22 Life Lessons to Change the Way You See the World

Aloneness
to
Oneness

22 Life Lessons to Change the Way You See the World

Todd Perelmuter

This book, which expounds upon the award-winning film of the same name and has impacted the lives of over 3 million people, is a roadmap back to rediscovering the truth of our infinite nature and infinite potential.

Aloneness: To discover the infinite peace that lies in solitude, stillness and silence. To realize the illusion of duality and to sense the presence of yourself in everyone and everything.

Oneness: The recognition that we are all deeply interconnected with each other and with the entire universe, from the stars we're made of to the energy that underlies all physical phenomena. It is to expand our awareness beyond the physical dimension and into the spiritual one. This isn't something to believe in, it's something we can all experience.

Aloneness to Oneness: There is no separate you, no separateness at all. There's only oneness. The difference between loneliness and aloneness is that loneliness happens when being alone causes suffering. Aloneness is the bliss that comes when you realize you are one with everything.

DEDICATION

For every single person who sensed there was more to life
than work, play, sleep, repeat. For everyone who felt that
there was a deeper reality than what we see on the surface.
For those who have touched their true nature beyond their
name, personality and physical body. For the ones called to
find a path of love, healing and peace.
This book is dedicated to you.

CONTENTS

Life Lesson 1

Spirituality Helps
When Nothing Else Can

During my travels in India, I met a man at an ashram. He was about 45 or 50, a little older than everyone else. I asked him what brought him to the ashram and he told me the story. A few years back, he retired from his job and decided to go traveling on a motorcycle with his wife on the back. One day, he pulled up to the front of a red light. Coming from behind them, a speeding truck ran into the back of his bike, killing his wife. He was badly injured and went into a coma for a few weeks.

When he came out of it, the doctors told him what had happened and that he wouldn't walk again. Naturally, he was devastated and heartbroken, and also physically broken.

He knew that the road ahead of rehabilitation — both physically and psychologically — was going to be hard.

He had a friend who was a yoga teacher who called him when she found out what happened to him. She told him, "Oh no no no. You're not going to stay in bed forever. We're going to get you started on the path to recovery."

Now this guy was a former professional baseball player and a biker. He thought yoga and spirituality were jokes. But, she came over anyway and wouldn't take "no" for an answer.

She taught him yoga which miraculously helped him walk again. Once he could walk and regain his ability to move around, he decided to travel to India and explore yoga more deeply.

While in India, he also started to learn about meditation, Hinduism and Buddhism. He told me that he never would have thought to go down this spiritual path, that he would have laughed at anyone who went to India to find themselves.

I asked if he got what he was hoping to find.

He looked in my eyes with intensity and clarity and said, "Losing my wife was the best thing that ever happened to me because it put me on this path."

He wasn't saying that he was glad she died. But he did recognize that before losing her, he didn't know how to truly enjoy or be present for his wife or his life.

Like most of us, he thought happiness comes from everything in life going right. What he learned was that it comes from within.

That is the power of spirituality. **It lifts us up when we are at our lowest, and it keeps us grounded when at our highest.**

The Spiritual Journey Begins

Before we dive straight in, we have to figure out what the word "spiritual" even means. To every person, it can mean something completely different.

For the sake of agreement, let's call it the nonphysical dimension. It is not the contents of our experience (thoughts, feelings, objects, our body, or other people), but the quality of our experience.

Beyond the ego, beyond the body and mind, it is the light of consciousness shining through. Beyond words, it's the energy underneath them. Beyond our life circumstances, it's where we are choosing to put our attention. Beyond desire, it's following our intuition. Beyond knowledge, it's wisdom.

We are already spiritual beings.

Asking how we can become spiritual is a lot like asking how to become human. We have this spiritual sense within us already.

The simple fact that we even can ask this question says that we, on some level, understand this spiritual nature within us. The fact that we all have this inherent spiritual craving means that there is a spiritual journey waiting for all of us.

Before celebrities, we worshiped deities. Before the dollar, we valued wisdom. This drive has always been with us. Like sex, food, water and safety, interconnected spiritual egolessness is our birthright. A state of pure being, nonattachment and oneness. Free from temporary and finite identification, and tapped into the eternal and infinite present moment.

Every single one of us has had moments and glimpses of enlightenment, inner peace, total wonder and awe.

That is our light of conscious awareness breaking through into view, even if only for a brief moment.

So we have to explore why we don't have this sensation all the time. What is it breaking through? And how can we hold onto it and experience it in a more lasting way?

The term "spiritual" has become an almost useless term as it means so many different things to different people.

So let's first define spiritual — so we know what we're talking about — as our psychological well-being and capacity for total peace, that feeling of pure love and light and joy that is based on nothing temporary, external, physical, or pleasurable. Just a steady feeling of endless gratitude and all the positive emotions.

And what we find when we explore the hindrances to that prolonged feeling is that we have these conditioned minds. Ever since birth, we have been constantly conditioned by the media, by friends and families, and by society as a whole, to believe certain things, to act in certain ways, and to have these similar thought patterns and processes as the rest of our culture.

Much of this cultural mind software is needed for civilization to survive and exist with all of the unique and diverse people living together. But if we lose focus of our true self/essence/beingness, then these mental societal constructs become pathways to unhappiness, mental health issues, and even physical issues such as pain, high blood pressure, weakened immune systems, and so many other stress-related physical ailments.

Think of the body like a rope. It can take quite a bit of tension and stress. But at a certain point, threads start to snap.

Humans are like this rope. Unhealthy food, chemical exposure, high impact exercise, physical and psychological trauma, stress, worry and fear all put strain on that rope. Healthy food, rest, light movement, meditation and relaxation all create slack. When the threads start to snap, we see skin problems, health problems, a weakened immune system, stiffness, pain, anxiety, depression, anger, addiction, etc...

So the key to becoming spiritual isn't that we do anything, it's the opposite — we have to undo everything.

We have to undo that rope altogether. We have to look at our thought processes that are creating the knots. We have to look at our conditioning, look at our belief systems — not only our religion, but how do we view ourselves? Do we feel that we're not good enough? That we always need to either acquire more or change ourselves more to be worthy? Is a lack of contentment underneath the need to constantly seek more? Or is it something else?

Is it this lack of contentment that is getting in the way of that presence and wonder we feel when we see a beautiful sunset? For the aurora borealis we become present, but for the miracle of ordinary life we pay it no mind. The more we can truly realize how complete and whole we are, how perfect we and this moment are, then we can let go of that constantly thinking mind that is full of incessant, repetitive thoughts, so often negative, and we can be at peace.

We can see the same thing we've seen a million times, and we can see it with newness, and wonder and beauty.

We can feel awe every moment, that gratitude for being alive and getting to experience this gift of life, to feel that we are not merely a tiny, insignificant part of this universe, not just some mistake, or random chance.

But we can feel that **we are the universe**, we can know, in every moment that we are those particles blasted off from a star, and we are deeply interconnected.

In this spiritual universe, there is a spiritual richness that we all have within us. **We can choose what we focus on.** We can rest our awareness. We are co-directors of this movie called life.

To direct one's attention with conscious intention is a remarkable ability we all have. Through meditation, we nurture and strengthen it.

We can choose to fixate on bad stuff, good stuff, or we can see how both are one and the same, how each moment of life is a miracle, how there are these invisible, interconnected relationships between all things, how everything is related and connected, and we can feel at peace and one with everything, while also being able to act in and engage with the world productively and mindfully.

By deepening our perspective to relationships over objects, conflict naturally disappears. Even in the middle of an argument, we can see how deeply connected we are with this other person, we can even in that moment feel peace and calm and compassion. We can discuss disagreements with love and compassion, and it is amazing what love and compassion can bring to a disagreement. Because both sides sense this energy flow of love between them, two people can share differing ideas, desires and opinions with zero anger or resentment.

It is the feeling of love that is the root of all spirituality. That is the mysterious force of the universe that binds us together, that holds the universe together, and that makes life worth living.

All we have to do is remove all those layers of the onion that is our mental conditioning so that we can get to the core of who we are, and touch that center and experience that pure love. We will then feel and know that we are spiritual beings at our very core.

How does spirituality improve our lives?

In some cultures, whatever the mind thinks is not even important. They only care about the gut and the heart. But in the West, in other parts of the world, and especially as places are modernizing, the brain has become a very valuable thing.

What can you create and produce and build and design — the mind is responsible for all these things. But our gut instinct or the heart's intuition, these things we inherently know deep down, are our truest and highest intelligence.

The mind can construct narratives that justify going against our own inner compass of compassion. The mind, because it's selfish, self-centered, and wants instant gratification, it will always try to talk us into the easiest thing. But if we let our heart lead, then our mind will follow, instead of the other way around.

This is how we can live in alignment, with no internal conflict, with inner harmony. Our mind will no longer sabotage our peace and happiness with disturbing thoughts of greed and vengeance.

By constantly living in the present moment, and constantly responding to what comes your way with presence and consciousness, is the only way that leads to a better future.

When your body is healthy, when your mind is clear, and when you are breathing properly, you're going to get high on life.

That's what spirituality is all about: getting peace, giving peace.

This is the circle of life. That's how it keeps spinning. When you're blessed, you pass it on to someone else because you know you are only blessed because someone helped show you the way. So it's important to receive and then pass it on.

For some people, spirituality is viewed as superstitious, fantastical, or the selfish pursuit of delusion. But science, reality and spirituality do not have to be mutually exclusive. We can explore and examine spirituality with meaningful and relevant questions. Such as, how can it be useful to me and society as a whole? What can logic and reason show us about that which seems illogical?

For me, spirituality comes down to living in our optimal psychological well-being. That's not to say it means the same thing as mental health. I don't mean healthy. I mean, joyful, loving and peaceful for no reason.

It means that the quality of whatever we experience in life

— the good and the bad — is present, patient, and peaceful. Science is all about quantity, and it cannot understand why human beings have a quality of having an experience. But if we take a scientific look at spirituality, we will see that quality is fundamental and paramount.

We are all spiritual beings in that we have a richness of inner experience and wisdom that we can all tap into. Everything we experience, even externally, happens within our own mind. But who and what and where is it that source of myself? Who is making our mental recreation of reality that happens beyond our control?

So self-inquiry and self-discovery in spirituality means to become conscious of our own consciousness — something vitally important that we almost never spend any time doing as a Western culture.

In this way, we raise our awareness, we expand our perspective, and we are able to allow greater wisdom, understanding, and thus a sense of peace to arise.

Stop trying to create something. We do that in our daily life all the time. What we have to do rather than create is to remove these layers of programming that society creates for us. These concepts hold us back, the identification with an identity.

When we remove all these layers of various concepts, what you have left is your true nature, your true identity, which is your infinite eternal consciousness, your awareness, pure consciousness.

When you take away all the thoughts, emotions, and physical body, you're left with pure awareness which is always there.

The thing I see people struggle with the most on their spiritually-seeking paths is almost a compulsion — an ego-driven desire — to achieve some high-like mental state, and that tends to make it much more difficult to reach a state of pure being, which is letting go of desire, letting go of concepts of enlightenment.

One of the earliest things that happens to almost everybody is we have a moment of pure bliss, egolessness, or timelessness in meditation — or it can appear out of the blue — but immediately the minds say, "That was amazing! What was that? I need more of that..." And just like that, the thinking mind starts up again and we're pulled out of that blissful presence.

It's very common. It's inevitable. It happens to everybody. Of course the mind is gonna say things like, "What is this incredible feeling? I'm gonna analyze it."

But spirituality is about letting go of everything we're holding onto.

It's letting go of our sense of identity and concepts and thoughts of how we feel about every little thing, and just being and experiencing. Not identifying as the experiencer or the experience, no subject or object, not even both or neither. It's recognizing there is only all as one. Everything we experience is filtered down through our brain and body to a single point of consciousness from which our perceptual awareness originates.

The true source of our life is our consciousness and awareness, without which we'd be a robot, a computer without an operator. We're living beings infused with this consciousness and when you can become aware of awareness, that's the higher consciousness and it's within you.

So instead of looking to the universe for a sign, look inward. Everything you need to know is within you.

There is nothing that Albert Einstein or Stephen Hawking or Mozart had that you don't have. All the answers lie within us. They say a teacher or guide will appear when you are ready, so keep your eyes open, stay aware, and be open. But never forget, our greatest guide and source of strength will always come from within.

Life Lesson 2

You Can't Stop Thinking by Focusing on Not Thinking

I remember joking with my friend in high school about how you can't think about not thinking. We noticed that the mind never stops and that you really can't think about nothing. That kind of mental puzzle plagued me for a long time.

There's a greater wisdom that comes when we're not clouded in thoughts, when we're not lost in thoughts, but when we're addressing exactly what's happening and not some mentally constructed simulation of what's actually happening.

It's impossible to think your way out of thinking.

All we can do is become fully present, which takes practice. When we are thinking, we are not present, but rather we are in our head. So we simply have to practice being fully aware with nonjudgmental curiosity about our surroundings and even our bodies. You can't stop thinking about something by focusing on not thinking about it. The only way to change your train of thought is to turn your attention toward that thought.

When we try to avoid something, we're giving it more weight and power.

When you try not to think about purple dolphins, it's all you're gonna think about.

So to stop dwelling in the past, don't resist it.

Just be aware of your thoughts, because once you become aware, you become present and you're watching the thoughts, you're not thinking with thoughts. And then pretty soon you stop that unconscious thinking naturally. That's the really cool stuff.

There is so much stuff happening within and around us at all times that we tend to tune out. We have to tune back in in order to find peace and freedom from our own mind. Thoughts will still pop up, but if we are aware of them, even then there will be peace.

They say that unconscious thinking and unconscious behavior cannot survive in the light of consciousness. The darkness of ignorance, which is ultimately a lack of awareness, cannot survive the light of consciousness. When we shine that light of conscious awareness on destructive and unconscious thinking, that unconscious thinking suddenly becomes conscious. Conscious thinking is deliberate, intentional, productive, skillful, self-aware, wise, useful, and harmonious.

But most of the day we're in autopilot mode, checking our phone constantly for no reason, losing our temper, giving into tempting food or some other vice, all unconsciously. Our brains turn whatever we do into habits if we keep doing them enough.

By becoming aware of ourselves and the things that we do, we can turn our unconscious reactions into conscious action. Instead of being a slave to our thoughts, our desires and our impulses, we become the master.

Instead of Trying to Stop Thinking, Try Sitting with Your Thoughts

Sitting with your thoughts is one of the most powerful spiritual practices there is. It is as simple as it sounds: to set aside some time to sit with your thoughts. During this time -- you can call it **Nothingness Meditation** -- you simply decide to witness your thoughts without acting on any impulse or urge no matter what. That's it.

Just witness your thinking mind. Witness how it thinks and all its clever tricks. Become super aware of how it tries to get us to do what it wants, which is always instant gratification because as a body-controlling software system, the mind always wants its needs met NOW. That's how these bodies will be most successful at surviving. Today, however, it's causing endless cravings and discontent.

During this transformative meditation practice, you become free from the slavery of your whims and desires.

Instead of feeling like any part of your life is out of control, you become the master of your mind and the conscious creator of your life.

When we are addicted from years of doing the same thing over and over again, every time we take part in that habit, we create neural pathways in the brain that make that action automatic and second nature.

In order to break any habit, any addiction, even the addiction to negative thinking, we need to create new neural pathways in the brain.

The way we do that, the way we create new habits, new, better choices, is to sit with our thoughts and to simply observe our impulses and urges, notice how they beat like a drum, louder and louder, louder and louder, to the point where we would normally give in to addiction, to an impulse, to our urges; instead of listening to our highest wisdom, our higher consciousness, and our true intentions.

So, as we watch those thoughts get louder and louder, in a safe, peaceful place like the meditation cushion, in a quiet, comfortable place where we don't feel stressed, where there's nothing else to do but listen to that urge.

Notice it doesn't actually control you. It can beat and bang as loud as it wants, and you are going to create a new pathway in the mind that says, I am stronger than these urges.

Every single time we witness the urge and don't act on it, that is our new habit that we are forming and strengthening every single time.

A daily meditation can be to simply sit, watch your thoughts, your urges, and your impulses, and really look

at them.

Don't just listen to them. Ask yourself, "What are these impulses, these voices in our heads? What are these urges that we have that are automated by our mind?" This heightened self-awareness becomes effortless because we've done it so many times that it's become natural. We can watch craving thoughts come, and we notice how they always go away. The mind always moves on.

The more we notice these urges come and go, the more we will learn that we don't have to act on them.

We become truly free, not only from whatever urge and impulse arises within us, but we are free from the effects of advertising. We are free from the effects that other people can have on our well-being and our psyche because we are stronger.

Then every passing thought, these little voices in our head, they come and go. Sometimes these thoughts in our head serve a purpose, sometimes they help us visualize our goals and help us solve problems using our creative energy. Sometimes, if not most, that voice in our head is negative. It is repetitive. It is incessant, and constant, and is not creating a better life for ourselves. It is not creating joy and peace within us.

The addicted brain is like a screaming baby seated next to us on a long flight. We can either choose to go crazy and fixate on the screaming, or, with proper wisdom, we can simply accept the situation and enjoy the comical nature of the moment. In the latter situation, you might be able to calm the baby yourself with some sweet smiles. In the former situation, the baby will surely find your restless energy unnerving.

Instead of Thinking Your Thoughts, Start Watching Them

Normally, **we don't watch our thoughts, we think our thoughts.**

And we think, "I am the thinker." In spirituality, we dig deeper. We recognize thought patterns and we observe how the mind actually works. We discover the nature of thoughts and our own mind. We practice being the silent witness of our thoughts so that negative thoughts don't disturb our peaceful witnessing presence. This can transform our entire lives.

How to observe our thoughts: Most of the time, in our day-to-day life, we are lost in thought. We are thinking thoughts, but we are not witnessing them. We are not watching or listening to them.

And most of the time, if we were to ask ourselves, "What was I thinking about a minute ago?" unless we've been obsessing about something all day, we'd have no idea what we were thinking about.

This stems from the illusion that we are our thoughts and that the voice in our head is who we truly are. If this is the case, there'd be no need to observe them because we are them, they are expressions of our deepest self.

And if we all have a voice in the back of our head, that we know is us, or we at least assume it is and we identify with it, then there would be no need to watch it or understand it because it is us and there would be no relationship there. But we do notice the separation.

We do notice that there is a thinker and a witness. There

is a conscious awareness that exists above thought. We say phrases like "my mind" and "my body" because we recognize that there is a relationship there between some fundamental essence of who we are, and the mind and body.

But as soon as we come to the realization that these thoughts are simply the egoic thinking part of our brain, just another part of us like how our hand is another part of us, then we become free from all self-blame, guilt and shame.

Our minds operate in a very specific way. Nothing arises in the field of our mental awareness out of nowhere. Everything is pulled from our subconscious and unconscious minds.

We cannot predict our next thought, we don't control what pops into our brain, we don't choose our urges. They are completely outside of our control and yet entirely within our responsibility.

Everything that our brains think up stems from our memories, stems from our physical and emotional state, and stems from what is happening around us that we may not even be consciously aware of.

Thoughts stem from this unconscious, dark, mysterious place of the mind. The unconscious and subconscious minds seep into our conscious awareness through thoughts, thoughts which we may or may not be conscious of having.

The more we realize that this ego — the thinking mind — is focused mainly on avoiding danger, surviving, and finding food and resources, the more we can understand how deeply rooted it is in fear and how it obsesses over negative experiences and is the cause for all the suffering in our lives.

In a modern, safe society, we don't need a hyper-vigilant

ego always looking for tigers and bears, and so today we create danger, anger and panic out of thin air. Instead of the occasional chest beating show of strength against a bear followed by rest and recovery, today we're in a subtle state of constant stress that is damaging our body.

So, we have to recognize two things:

1. Our thoughts are not who we are. These are not the thoughts we would think if we were thinking consciously with our greatest intention, which would be of course to think things that generate feelings of peace and joy, and loving emotions.

2. These thoughts often cause a great deal of suffering and actually need to be watched, observed and monitored very closely.

The key to observing our thoughts is disidentifying with them and re-identifying with the witness.

There aren't two selves inside each of us. There isn't an observer of our thoughts and the thinking mind itself. Thoughts are simply mental formations that can be perceived by consciousness, our true self. Like sounds and sights, smells and tastes, touch and bodily sensations, thoughts are just another thing we can perceive. I am not my eyes, I am the one who sees. And like so, we are not the mind, we are the watchers.

Perceptual forms, whether they are objects that we perceive with our fingers, our eyes, our ears or our mind, such as the things we experience as we go about our daily life; or the forms we see when we turn our attention inward, close our eyes, and observe our thoughts, observe our feelings and sensations within our body; these forms all arise within our conscious field of awareness.

Most of the time, while we are going about our day-to-day activities, we are lost in thought or we are distracting ourselves with our phone.

We are usually unaware of our thoughts, unaware of how they are negative, repetitive, and often mindlessly narrating whatever is happening around us, which in fact, makes us unable to see reality as it really is.

Instead of letting whatever happens exist as it is, we create a one-sided story in our mind that sees everything as either good or bad (duality).

Often, we see the negative in everything because that is what these are designed to look out for, so that we would stay away from wolves, not go too close to cliffs, and be weary of any risks and dangers in the natural world.

Naturally, these thinking machines inside of us are going to fixate and obsess over anything negative that they can latch on to. It will imagine the worst dangers, the most frightening scenarios. And oftentimes, the worst possible imagined future.

So, we first have to become aware of the tricks that the mind plays. We have to be aware that we're not in danger, that these fears are all in our head. Of course, if you're camping in the woods, or if you're in a dangerous neighborhood at night, you might need to listen to that inner threat warning.

But most of the time, when we're relaxing, or we're at work, or we're stuck in traffic, that negative voice goes into overdrive because it doesn't know the difference between stress from a job and stress from a tiger. So we can easily find ourselves going down these negative downward spirals, horrible trains of thought that we can't get ourselves out of because our whole body state is in a fight or flight stress response.

Oftentimes, when we have prolonged fight or flight mode, and we're not fighting because we live in a civilized society, and we're not fleeing because there is no actual physical danger, this often is what turns into depression, which is kind of a third survival stress response to fighting and fleeing — playing dead.

This third stress-response is hardwired into us. This is why when we get depressed, we feel unable to get out of bed and unable to do anything, even though we know we should.

Even though people are trying to get us out of it, nothing can because we are in this natural state of essentially playing dead as a survival tactic.

When fight or flight hasn't been able to help us because it's not a socially acceptable response, we naturally want to hibernate 'til it's over.

So, before I get into what we can do about breaking free from that mental cyclone, a lot of people wonder why our brains are wired like this. Are we defective? Why have we been made so dysfunctionally?

And the answer, of course, is: we are not defective. We just have a survival mechanism working in overdrive that is no longer necessary in modern society.

The fact of the matter is that we were evolving into modern humans while we were living in the wild. Fight, flight, and freeze were appropriate stress responses. We didn't have iPads and smartphones and TV and film and music and video games and all of these attention industries. No board games, card games, or newspapers. No jobs, no bills, no pubs. There was nothing to distract us so we were able to naturally rest and relax and be witness to our thoughts.

In fact, it's believed that before modern agriculture, we would hunt and forage for food for only 4 hours a day. The rest was leisure time. Then, when civilizations and modern farming practices came about, more and more food was needed for more and more people, and humans became enslaved to their fields.

In the earliest days of modern man, meditating was a natural thing to do back then. We lived in tight-knit communities, there was no crime (there was nothing to steal), and we would dance and sing around the fire. If there was a moment of stress, an elephant nearby, a forest fire, or a challenging hunt, there was always plenty of time to allow the body to rest and recover from that stress response.

Without magazines and books and iPod Shuffles, there was no escaping their thoughts and feelings. So, they were all highly reflective, contemplative and meditative.

This would lead to everyone reaching extreme heights of wisdom and expanded consciousness. They would surely identify with the witnessing presence of their thoughts and feelings and not with the thoughts and feelings themselves, for they are fleeting yet consciousness remains.

This massive free time — like how all animals enjoy, relax and play — allowed ancient people a much greater sense of peace and contentment than we have today.

All because they were fully present. They were not dreaming of being in Paris or having the corner office, driving Ferraris or scoring Taylor Swift tickets. There was nowhere else to be and nothing else to do. According to modern society, ancient tribes had nothing. Yet to them, they had everything. It's modern people who have everything and yet feel they have nothing.

Being fully present, fully relaxed, yet fully alert, used to be our natural state of being. It is also every animal's state of being.

A deer may have a moment of stress if there is a predator nearby, but it will always immediately go and shake off the stress. As its natural baseline state of being, the deer is always alert yet relaxed.

This is the steady, centered state of meditation — not too lazy, not too tense, just calm and aware. Once we become free from the conditioning of society, this becomes our natural state again.

Just because we live in the age of endless entertainment and distractions, we can get back to that state. So how do we start observing our thoughts?

There are two ways and both are essential for maintaining a sense of peace and happiness through life's ups and soon-to-be-ups (downs).

1. Close Your Eyes and Turn Your Attention Inward

The first step, and most powerful, is to close your eyes and turn your attention inward for some period of time, every day if you are able to. It can be for a few hours or a few minutes. It can even be as simple as not taking your phone into the bathroom with you, which apparently is something we've all become accustomed to. Whenever and wherever you can have a moment of peace and quiet.

Then, you'll close your eyes if that's possible, block out all of the distractions if there are any, and turn 100% of your focus inward and simply watch your thoughts.

Don't try to think of anything specific. Don't try to do anything at all. Just allow for whatever comes up to come up.

After a moment or so, turn your focus to your breath. Feel all of the sensations of breathing — the in and out breaths. It sounds easy but most new meditators will not be able to focus on their breath for more than a few breaths. One thing that can help is to count breaths in your head.

When your mind naturally wanders, before turning your attention back to your breath, make a little note in your mind if you can of what you were just thinking about, what distracted you in the first place, and how the train of thought went from us getting distracted to catching ourselves.

See if you can remember and figure out how you got on to what you were thinking about. Maybe you heard a noise like a bell, and it reminded you of the microwave and you started thinking about what you're going to eat next. Maybe you were thinking, "This is so boring, I can't wait 'til I'm doing X, Y, and Z."

It can even be something as simple as noticing how much you hate meditation. That is totally fine and normal at first because we've been conditioned 24/7 since birth to run away as fast as we can from this perfect and peaceful present moment. Whatever thoughts come up, allow them to be, don't judge them, simply take note. The thinking mind wants to judge and label everything. Awareness simply observes, with neutrality so that it can see reality. As soon as a judgment is placed on a thought, or on any experience, we get further away from that experience. While it's natural for the mind to judge, our greater wisdom knows that **there is good and bad *in* everything, but where we put our focus *is* everything.**

All you have to do is watch any debate and know that people can talk for hours about completely opposite points of view. So that means that people's thoughts have nothing to do with what is true or false, right or wrong. To understand reality, we must recognize the deeper truths beyond our thinking mind.

Every thing contains everything, and anything can be said about just about anything. Many newscasters on those 24-hour news channels know all about this. They can have almost no information about an event and they will talk for 12 hours straight about it, just guessing and opining, because that's their job. This is like the nature of the mind. It will think. It is a thinking machine. Thinking is its job.

The more we watch the mind, the more we create a distance between the mind's contents and who we truly are — consciousness itself. The greater that distance, the broader our perspective becomes, the more we can see the big picture, and from this expanded consciousness a greater wisdom, patience and peaceful detachment emerge.

The thinking mind can only think one word at a

time in our heads. Whereas consciousness is able to perceive so much information at once: the complexity of music, the geometrically precise recreation of all the visual information our eyes take in, billions of pixels, such intricate sounds and smells and tastes all at once, and an instant recognition of every object exactly for what it is, with instant estimations of mass and texture, speed and location, as well as the meanings and purposes of everything we see.

The one-word-at-a-time mind is very limited, but we have a higher wisdom. That wisdom is the witness that observes our thoughts and is able to choose which thoughts to act on, and which thoughts to ignore. That is what I mean by our highest consciousness and our highest wisdom.

The more distance we create between the witness — our true selves — and the thinker, the quieter those thoughts become.

And, the more peaceful life becomes.

When we identify as the thinker, and there is no distance between us and our thoughts, it is like a screaming person in our head and we become much more impulsive. We are much more likely to act on every desire and every impulse that pops into our head.

The more distance we create simply from observing thoughts nonjudgmentally without reacting to those thoughts, we become wiser and have a great understanding of ourselves as well as the minds of others. All scientific inquiry is about observation and gathering knowledge. So what we are doing is witnessing and observing our mind to gain understanding and wisdom into how it works and how we can get it to work better for us.

The more time we spend with our eyes closed in meditation, and the more time we spend observing our thoughts, the more that distance grows and grows, and the more that voice gets quieter and quieter. Eventually, like a samurai on guard protecting his people, no matter what we will remain alert yet calm, aware yet relaxed, present yet prepared.

Just like how a child who's being watched is on their best behavior, the more we watch our thoughts, and the more we make that a habit, the more it will stop acting out unconsciously and unintentionally. It will sit up straight, be quiet, speak only when adding value to the situation, and it will be more peaceful and cooperative. If we root ourselves in positive conscious intentions, our minds will generate peace, joy and compassion for us.

2. Make Observing Your Thoughts a Daily Habit

The second thing we have to do to observe our thoughts, beyond closing our eyes and turning our attention inward, is to convert that into our daily practice which becomes part of our everyday life, and that becomes a habit even when we're not closing our eyes.

The way we do that is whenever we're doing anything, especially things that are laborious and bothersome, we do a **mindfulness mental checkup**. This is simply putting our attention on our thoughts, emotions, and our physical body as well, and taking notes. Are our faces scrunched up and we're looking mad while we do the dishes or cook food? Or are we relaxed, joyful and peaceful? And we don't need a mirror to recognize this, we can feel from within if we're keeping tension in our face, we can sense if our shoulders are hunched over and contracted, or if we're open and relaxed. This is so important because so much of our mental state is reflected in our physical body, and by understanding this mind-body connection we break free from the false sense of duality and separateness that exist within us.

We all agree that certain emotions can give us frown lines, but there are still many people who do not understand that stressful emotions can create physical problems like IBS, ulcers, fibromyalgia, arthritis, carpal tunnel syndrome, plantar fasciitis, chronic pain and more. Not to mention the mental health conditions caused by stress and negative emotions, like depression and anxiety. So many people are suffering today because we ignore the mind-body connection — how the mind affects the body and how the body affects the mind.

Once we've checked the body for stress, we turn our attention to our emotional and mental states. What are our thoughts doing? Are they complaining or joyful? Are they weaving an intricate story of injustice, anger and vengeance targeting the whole world for FORCING ME TO DO THE DISHES WHEN I HATE DOING THE DISHES?!?!?! Or, are the thoughts lovely and kind and beautiful and grateful and positive? Are we thanking the Earth for these incredible blessings of convenience and luxury, of running water and a clean home?

We humans are a funny species, aren't we? We could literally be given God powers, a genie's lamp, and the adulation of the entire world, and two weeks later we'd be bored, complaining and ungrateful.

Mindfulness Mental Checkups have never been more essential than they are today because of all the time we spend on social media or watching film and television. So much in the media is negative and this influx of constant content will naturally make the voice in our head more negative too if we are not mindful of it.

Now I'm not saying we have to toss out our favorite horror movies, true crime series, and news channels. A lot of people love being in a stress response, but also we might want to release that a little so as not to give ourselves any back pain. And it's important to take note of what content we're consuming, because we only watch what resonates with our mental state. When we're kids, we vibe only with kid shows. If we're only vibing with murder mysteries, it's worth exploring why and how that may affect us.

It's very important that we spend as much time looking within as we do paying attention to what's outside of us.

If we can do a 50-50 split, where we're looking through social media and we're scrolling and we're paying attention and engaged, but we also have 50% of our attention on our own thoughts, how we're reacting emotionally, and how our body is responding.

This is what we call total awareness. We're aware

of what we're doing, we're aware of where we are putting our awareness, and we're aware of the quality of our awareness — if it's broad and diffused like a lamp, or focused and sharp like a laser beam.

Total awareness is the key to not only maintaining conscious awareness of our thoughts and emotions throughout the day, but this is how we can remain present and mindful our whole life and participate in the world. We don't have to go live in a cave or a forest to learn this. **The world is our school, life is the lesson.**

This is the key to enlightenment, which is to live in the state of constant present-moment awareness, where we enjoy the pleasures of the world but we never get lost in them. They don't consume us, and we instead consume them with mindfulness. In this way, we can enjoy everything.

We can enjoy the pleasures when they come. We can even enjoy them as they leave. Things change, and there will be pain and difficulty. We can remain mindful during those times too. All we have to do is close our eyes, turn inward, and give 100% of our attention to the way these crazy things called brains work.

Then, throughout the day, by maintaining awareness and being aware of our thoughts whenever our mind wanders, our level of awareness grows higher and higher, our consciousness expands evergreater, and by mastering our mind, we master our lives.

How to Think More Positive Thoughts

Why does our mind betray us? Why does it cause so much suffering? Why does it embark upon downward spirals of seemingly inescapable negative thinking? And most importantly, why is it harder to believe positive thoughts than negative ones? Why don't we ever get to go on upward spirals of joy?! Why are negative thoughts so powerful? And how can we begin to shift our focus away from negativity and towards peace and gratitude? Let's explore.

Thoughts only have power over us if we believe they are us.

If we believe that this voice inside of us is our true self, then by that very nature, we would listen to whatever pops into our brain as though it was our ultimate truth. But we all know that our brain can sometimes think some pretty crazy things that we don't always act on.

So, there is this higher intelligence and wisdom beyond thoughts — the conscious awareness that perceives our inner and outer life.

It doesn't think or know anything, but it observes with neutrality and so it understands everything.

When we think nonstop without a break, we get so lost in our thoughts and what we're doing that we lose ourselves in the present moment.

Instead of looking with our awareness, we are lost in a fantasy. Our vision is obscured and we are no longer present. We are essentially robots, in autopilot mode, prone to mistakes and accidents. Our mind, trying to help, ends up working against us. Instead of this internal fighting, we need our awareness and intellect to work together.

Thoughts are loud and clear, but they are a tiny fraction

of the inner workings of our minds, like waves on top of the ocean. Our unconscious and subconscious minds are like the vast ocean underneath the surface. Thoughts can give us a hint as to what's going on beneath the surface of our psyche, but we have to learn how to listen.

In the unconscious and subconscious minds, when there is repressed and suppressed anger or hatred or self-loathing or low self-esteem, then the thoughts that bubble up to the surface and enter the realm of conscious thoughts may reflect that underlying current of negative energy.

Our thoughts may be self-critical, critical of others, and complaining in nature. Or, they can be boastful, prideful, superior and self-righteous in order to mask our insecurity from ourself.

So why do we have all this negativity inside us? This is because deep down we are resisting life itself and what is happening around us. Because we have this ego in our mind that identifies with our legal name and this persona that we have created.

The ego gets stronger by identifying as being for or against any issue, and by creating a strong position in opposition to, or in favor of, whatever is happening within and around us.

The thinking mind (AKA the ego, these thoughts in our head, the endless stream of thoughts) is like a social media algorithm that only shows you content designed to infuriate you in order for you to comment and engage in debate.

The ego knows that if it can get you worked up about something, then it can get you lost in thought for hours. We'll freely ride with our ego on a downward spiral of negativity, through an endless stream of obsessive, compulsive, incessant thinking over some imagined offense or perceived slight. The ego will use anything it can to jump to conclusions and get us all worked up and stirred up. That nonstop stream of thought will cling on to anything even remotely negative that it can get its hands on.

So when we are in this negative state, when our thoughts are negative, we can't force ourselves to think happy thoughts. We have to understand what is at the root of this mental state. We have to dig deep down into our subconscious mind through meditation.

We need time for reflection, contemplation, and self-inquiry to weed out those seeds of anger and negativity.

If we plant and nurture those positive seeds of love and gratitude, and we water them with kindness and compassion, our thoughts will naturally be peaceful and joyful.

But whether your thoughts are joyful or negative, it's important to be mindful of both and to try to maintain equanimity through good thoughts and bad thoughts. Bring peace and spaciousness to your thoughts and feelings, allowing them to be exactly as they are. Root out thoughts stemming from ignorance, fear and anger. Listen to the thoughts that align with your highest intentions and greatest good.

Life Lesson 3

There is No Beginning or End

When we see movies, they always have a beginning and end. But in every movie, something happened before the movie started, we just don't see it. At the end, we see the wedding or the big victorious moment, and then the credits roll.

But in reality, those characters will all have to go on and live out the rest of their days. And so, with our ubiquitous media presenting us with these neat little stories wrapped up in pretty bows for us, we then fall for the illusion that things have beginnings and ends, here one minute and gone the next.

For a long time, physicists believed that there was a beginning to the universe. Only now are they beginning to say there might have been something before that. The truth is, space is infinite and time eternal — beginningless and endless change.

Birth and death are illusions. There is no beginning and there is no end. Before this life, we were alive in our parents. And before that we were alive in our grandparents, and our ancestors before that.

One thing gets passed on to another, one form changes into another, and the same as in death, our energy passes on.

From animals consuming life by eating plants, to creating life by giving birth, and from energy transforming into matter and matter into energy, the universe is no more than an interplay of cosmic energy. And like the art of dance, it is only a present moment phenomenon.

Albert Einstein once said, "The distinction between past, present and future is only a stubbornly persistent illusion." He believed from his studies that time is not real. And yet, not only do most of us believe in the illusion of time, we live imprisoned in the illusion of time.

So often, we put off our current happiness for some imagined future. We believe we should suffer now but later, once we've achieved our goals, then we'll be happy, only to find that we're still unhappy.

The truth is, time is not real. Time did not get born, time will never die. Things only change forms.

Time is human beings' futile attempt at trying to hold on to the past or escape to the future. It's a desperate attempt at stability, solidity and control in an ever-changing universe.

There is no past and there is no future. There is only now.

Time is a measurement. It is as real as a centimeter. We use time merely to measure change — the Earth's rotation, an atom's vibration, etc... A clock is nothing more than a tape measure. But, ever since humans started farming, and thus needed to prepare early for future harvests, we started living in time. This is when the suffering began. This is when it became less important to be present in order to find food, and it became more important to be in time — planning, recording, and storing. Farming was the first time-based profession that led to all others. Today, we spend most of our lives in the past or the future, and we can no longer see the peace and beauty of the here and now.

While the human brain is amazing at thinking, we've thought ourselves into a trap of suffering.

But by understanding this simple basic truth, we can consciously evolve towards a mind that both honors the past and future, while residing in the joyful peace right now.

The closer we look at time, the more we recognize it as an illusion. Time is a construct of the human brain's capacity to have memory and remember the past, and to imagine and anticipate a future.

If we lost the ability to remember the past, we would actually see reality clearer. There is only the present moment, there is only a continuous stream of presence.

Everything that ever happened in the past happened in, what was at the time, the present moment. Everything that will ever happen, will happen in the present moment. That's all there is. Everything else is illusion caused by clinging and grasping, or aversion and avoidance.

We all get attached to certain people, objects, ideas and situations. And yet, every single thing changes. If we are flexible, we'll bend. If we are rigid, loss can break us.

By understanding this Law of Constant Change on a deep level, we won't be surprised when surprising change happens to us. We won't waste time needlessly obsessing over loss because we'll be present and aware of what is happening now instead.

Even though we know that these bodies start to decay the moment we're born, we don't see this decay. We see what seems like a permanent, unchanging person. We don't see the growth of plants or animals happen before our eyes. We only notice the aging when we think back or look at an old photograph.

Because everything around us looks stable, it creates a deception that things last forever. While we know conceptually that that's not true, on a subconscious level we expect things and people to last forever, exactly the way they are. But upon closer inspection, we'll see that people are changing constantly.

Thoughts and emotions are changing constantly. Our dreams and fears and tastes are changing constantly. Our cells are dying and new ones are being reborn constantly. The more we meditate on this impermanent nature of everything and allow it to seep down into our subconscious, if we simply observe our own constantly changing thoughts, constantly coming and going, then we're better able to recognize that everything is in this state of change.

In this state of expanded conscious awareness that goes beyond the illusion of time, not only will death not seem so unbearable, but we will not even see it as an end because we will understand that there is no beginning and there is no end. There are only changes, changes in form and the flows of energy. Nothing is created, nothing destroyed. There is no single moment of death that we can pinpoint. It is a gradual process, a shift.

When we realize that there's no single moment we're born, there's no single moment we die, we become free from the binary delusion of duality.

When we realize that everything exists because of some cause and effect, that the seeds of the past are blossoming now, and that the future is being planted today, then we can take peace and solace in the fact that nothing's ever gone. There is only the endless cycle of change, death and rebirth, all happening right now.

There is Only Transformation

Beginnings and ends are fictions perpetuated by Hollywood's perfectly neat little stories that have these clear starts and endpoints. The truth is, real life is beginningless and endless. We may think of birth as a beginning and death as an ending, but life was here before we arrived and it will continue on after us.

This is true even according to the laws of physics. Nothing begins and nothing ends because nothing can be created or destroyed. There is only change. The nature of all things is eternal transformation.

We are made of the cosmos. We are every lifeform that came before us. When we notice that our bodies age, our thoughts and feelings constantly change, and yet our consciousness is unchanging and everpresent, we begin to realize that eternal and infinite nature within us. We recognize the truth of change, we discover that we were never born and we will never die, and that we only change forms and dimensions.

The first law of thermodynamics is that energy cannot be created or destroyed, it can only change forms. So the total amount of energy and matter in the Universe remains constant, merely changing from energy to matter and matter to energy.

Before you were born, you existed in your parents as an egg and sperm. You existed in your grandparents before that and your great grandparents before that. You are the seed of a process that began before the Big Bang and your existence will ripple into the cosmos forever into the future.

We are the eternal, nonmaterial energy that leaves our body when we die and makes us who we are. It does not exist in the dimension of spacetime. Because of its constant unchanging presence, we are able to perceive the perception of stillness. Our mental camera of consciousness is always here and now, witnessing the ever-changing experience of our lives. And even though we know that change is the ultimate truth, we still resist, fear, and fight it.

We may not have the path laid out for us, but it is ours to discover.

The entire cycle of life is beautiful. We can't pick and choose one part to love and one part to hate because no part can exist without the whole. We cherish a flower because we know it is fleeting.

To fear death is to fear birth and all of life.

A tiger killing a gazelle is not a sad event. A gazelle dying of old age is not sad. Plants dying in the cold of winter is not sad. These are essential to the process of life.

There is no death, and there is no birth, there is only the constant change of form because life is eternal.

A human being consists of more microbial organisms than human cells. We are kept alive by other living beings. We are nurtured by nature, and in turn we nurture nature.

We are not separate people with separate thoughts. We are one life, everyone playing out their role perfectly. We may see people as bad, but the truth is that every single person is their inescapable karma (cause and effect).

Like a tree, we humans aren't meant to reach the sun. The point is simply to grow.

In this perfect magical world that we are all born into as helpless mutes, there were trees with delicious fruits waiting for us to enjoy. There are trees to build houses, fire to keep warm, fresh water rains down from the sky, and everything we need is here waiting for us in abundance. The sun will spectacularly cross the horizon twice a day and the stars will blow your mind wide open. There's honey and flowers and puppies and rainbows and we have these incredible bodies and brains!

The signs are everywhere: this is a loving universe. We must also trust that the universe doesn't make mistakes and that the process of birth and death is nothing to fear. They are not accidents.

They are equally beautiful processes of transformation.

We will never be born and we will never die because the universe was never born and will never die. There is only change. The shape of the ocean changes constantly, but it can't disappear. Even the water that evaporates, it goes somewhere, it becomes rain, then rivers, then ocean again. It all changes all the time. Before every beginning, there was something. After every ending, a new beginning.

The more we understand on a deep level this impermanence, this temporary nature of all things, the more peace and joy we can bring to every situation, no matter how bad or how difficult.

We can still have goals and work to achieve things, but we're no longer attached to the outcome nor fixated on some end result. We are fully in the present moment. All of our attention is on the task at hand so that we can perform better, so that we can do what needs to be done now in order to create a brighter future ahead.

Life Lesson 4

Change is the Only Constant

We all get attached to certain people and forms and ideas and situations. The truth is though, all these things will forever change.

And yet, we still develop attachments, ultimately leading to our inevitable suffering. So, how do we break free from the grip of attachments while still forming strong, healthy and loving bonds?

Nearly all suffering is because we forget the Law of Constant Change. Ever since the Big Bang — as far back as we can observe — in every single moment of time and in every single point of space, there has been endless change.

No two moments are alike. The universe is expanding, every atom vibrating, every particle spinning, every thought coming and going until the end of time. We cling to temporary phenomena, like sand falling through our fingers as we try to hold on futilely to anything solid or permanent.

Becoming rooted and grounded, centered and balanced, doesn't come from false permanence or resisting change. It comes from flowing and changing with the change happening all around us.

This law of change underscores every single aspect of our existence. Our heart is beating, blood is pumping, electrical signals are firing, and every one of your favorite electronics will either break or go missing.

While sometimes change happens slowly, and sometimes so slowly we don't see it, such as a piece of fruit rotting or a plant growing, or a building deteriorating, these things that happen over days, weeks, months years, our own growth even, because we don't see it happening before our eyes, we fall for the illusion that there is permanence, stagnation, stability, repetition and sameness.

The illusion of permanence is the cause of all human suffering.

Illusory permanence causes boredom because it compares the present moment to the past and the future, making us fail to see the vibrant newness of each moment. Things may appear similar on the surface, but in reality every moment is completely new. Our viewpoint is always changing, light is always changing, sounds are always changing, and our bodies and minds are always changing.

When we live in false permanence, we see labels instead of objects. We see names instead of people. We fear we'll lose what we have and never get what we seek. Instead of abundance, we feel lack.

We're always comparing and competing, and our desperate attempt to cling onto permanence only masks our fear of loss, our fear of change, and our fear of death.

This fear keeps us in a state of heightened stress, which makes us prone to costly mistakes, poor health, a lack of focus and mental illness.

The more we understand this Law of Change, the more we can overcome any negative mood, feeling or situation because we know deep down that nothing lasts forever.

The more we fully reflect on this law and understand it, think about it, talk about it, and make it a second-nature way of seeing the world, then no temporary circumstance can ever be too daunting or unbearable.

And the good news is, every circumstance is temporary.

No circumstance will be overwhelming or cause negative emotions because we will know that any fleeting thought-form, emotion, or displeasing situation is only here for a brief minute. Then, it's gone forever. It only lives on if we are attached to it. If we thought it had some significant importance, then we can end up carrying that moment with us for the rest of our lives. Eventually, the accumulation of so many bad moments on our shoulders will break us.

We need to constantly remind ourselves at every chance if we get that **this moment is only here for this moment and then it is gone.** This frees us to live life to the fullest, to cherish every moment while simultaneously never getting attached to, or resisting, any moment because we are simply flowing with time. We appreciate the beauty we see in the world, and we can allow whatever is displeasing to flow by without disturbance, constantly welcoming the moment and letting it go, and leaving the past in the past.

Accepting the Uncertainties of Life

The only thing certain in life is uncertainty. Try as we might, there are too many variables for any one of us to accurately predict the future.

Even if we could predict the future, having knowledge of the future would change our behavior and choices, thus changing the future.

So it's impossible to know the future because knowing the future would change the future and so the prediction would turn out not to be true.

And that's the beauty — we're not supposed to know. Not knowing allows us to live fully in this moment, to be present for our lives, and to appreciate whatever happens to come into our field of consciousness for however long or brief it may be.

This mysterious, unknowable future does not need to lead to stress, anxiety, uneasiness or fear. No matter what comes our way, with presence we will be able to handle it in the moment with peace, clarity and calm.

We don't need to be optimists or pessimists. We don't have to cling on to hope or fear despair. We can embrace the great unknown, we can see the beautiful mystery of life without needing answers, and we can accept an uncertain future. This is what it means to see reality as it truly is, free from delusion, and free from the bonds of concepts.

What in this life is certain? We are guaranteed not one

more breath, and yet every single moment is infused with the miracle and joy of life.

It's easy to become so obsessively focused, constantly worrying about some imagined future that may or may not come. When we do this for too long, we miss out on the joy of living because we've been living in anticipation of some future moment, in some imagined future, lost in our own thoughts, trapped in the mental stories we tell ourselves about how things should be. And then, whenever the unexpected does happen in our life, we respond with fear, panic, and stress.

But if we can embrace our highest intentions in the present moment, if we can put all our focus into right now, towards building today what we wish to achieve tomorrow, without attachment to the outcome, then we will be free from any fear of uncertainty. All that remains is a confidence that whatever comes up in this moment, we can handle and rise to the occasion.

Attachment to the outcome and obsession with some imagined future means that you are mentally resisting each task that will help you reach your desired future. You're not present. You're mindless about what you're doing. And what you're doing is creating stress and dissociation in your life. More likely than not, if you're working from a place of fear, you're unconsciously manifesting your nightmare scenario.

If you create a clear positive vision that you wish to happen, and then you set out on making it happen with your full presence, success is best assured.

When you completely set aside that future goal so you can focus on the steps to reach there, there is no destination you can't reach.

Any speed bump or unexpected detour can simply be assessed at the time it arises, again with our full presence, our full awareness and our higher wisdom, all because we have made a practice of taking on things that come up in the moment, head on, with zero resistance, zero negativity and zero stress. We simply rise to the occasion, step up to the plate, and take each tiny little moment head-on.

Moment by moment, nothing is overwhelming and nothing too great to bear. With present moment conscious awareness combined with deep rooted intention, the answers will present themselves exactly when needed.

These are definitely uncertain times, but if we waste this moment worrying about the future, then we will find ourselves living in a future that will have happened to us, rather than one we have created with conscious intention. Those are two very different futures.

Letting Go of Our Attachment to Impermanence

If we look around us, things look permanent, solid and stable. Only when we can see years of change, by looking at an old photo for instance, can we see the decay and impermanence.

In my book, *Death, Life and Oneness: Spiritual Wisdom From the Gita*, I included a relevant excerpt from the Bhagavad Gita:

> All pleasure that arises from sensory objects can ultimately only bring about suffering. Though appearing as enjoyable to worldly-minded people, they have a beginning and an end, they come and go. It is for this reason that a wise man does not indulge in them. He alone who is able to withstand this very

life before casting off his body and the urges of lust and anger, is a yogi, and he alone is a happy man.

Here, the Gita shows us that the root cause of suffering is our attachment to impermanence, attachment to temporary material forms and sense perceptions.

We think we suffer because of some external situation. But suffering doesn't exist outside of ourselves.

All suffering is rooted in the mind. It is a mental creation, stemming from our craving for temporary phenomena, whether it's money, possessions, experiences, or relationships.

Human beings wish for everything good to last forever and nothing bad to ever happen. But the fact of the matter is, everything changes all the time. There is not a single thing that doesn't change. Everything follows the laws of physics, things are constantly changing form, from matter to energy, and energy to matter. Things are decaying, and that decay leads to rebirth. But because we don't see the constant cycle of death and rebirth taking place before our very eyes, we get surprised and shocked when things change.

But when we understand on a deep level that everything is fleeting, that nothing bad lasts and nothing good lasts either, then we make peace with reality. No matter what comes into our life, and no matter what leaves our life, we remain at peace. Because we understand the law of impermanence, we understand the fleeting nature of reality.

When we expect a perfect life, we'll fall apart when things don't go our way. And when they do go our way, we won't appreciate life's blessings because we felt entitled to them. But when we expect chaos, we will be at peace with chaos and grateful whenever it pauses.

Objects, situations and experiences don't make us happy anyway.

We can look at a simple bite of chocolate cake for evidence of this. If you like chocolate cake, and let's assume we all like chocolate cake, when it's in our mouth for a few seconds, we feel great pleasure. As soon as that bite is over though, we crave another bite.

If we give in to that temptation, pretty soon we feel sick and bloated because we ate that whole cake. Or, if we don't have that second bite or third slice, then we are tormenting ourselves and longing for that chocolate cake. But the cake, our favorite thing in the world, didn't bring lasting joy. This is the nature of everything in our universe.

There is the yin and yang in every experience. There is the good and bad in pleasurable things. It comes from craving, desire, wanting and longing. It completely disturbs our mental peace. If stuff made us happy, each bite would make us happier and happier and we would never stop.

But everything that we ever found pleasurable, we have stopped. That is the cycle of things. There is newness and excitement, then boredom and seeking again. This is why new phones and computers come out every year.

Similarly, unpleasurable things create suffering because we resist them and wish for them not to be happening. We fight with reality — a losing battle — by creating a mental aversion to the unpleasurable experience.

If we examine closely though, we'll find it's never the things that upset us. At the root, it is our expectation for a perfect life, permanently.

Change is the nature of things. The temporary forms that appear within our field of consciousness bear little importance on the quality of our lives. It is our response to those things that will determine the quality. If we react to undesirable situations with anger, we'll be angry. If we respond with calm and compassion, our lives will be filled with love and joy.

When we meditate on the constantly changing nature of reality, when we meditate on our attachment to temporary phenomena, fleeting objects and brief experiences, we begin to notice that it is the attachment that creates the suffering.

Never before in human history have so many people expected their whole life to be peaceful and easy. While I wish this for everyone, we know that change is the one constant in this physical universe. When we expect the good and the bad, we accept reality and we can take it all in, hold space for it, and see it with peace and equanimity.

Permanence is an illusion. Attachment is a delusion.

Whatever is temporary is only an illusion. It's here one minute and gone the next, like a magic trick. Every physical thing in our lives is temporary, yet we spend so much time obsessing over these illusory perceptions. Understanding impermanence on a deep level rids the mind of any ability to experience loss, grief, sorrow, and attachment. Only the infinite empty space, the eternal present moment, and the light of consciousness are permanent and unchanging. That is what's real. That is worth focusing on.

Life Lesson 5

There's Never Enough Stuff

As a former ad man in New York, I had a firsthand look into how marketing and advertising works, how it creates demand, and how it influences people to want products they would never normally want. I was both responsible and susceptible for a lot of that. I finally reached a point when I realized that if I was going to continue down the road I was going, I would never be happy. I realized, there's always a new clothing style, always a new technology, and always some new product that is alluring and enticing.

More money. More clothes. More luxury items. More cars.

Vacations. Nicer home. Nicer furniture. We all know the feeling of wanting something, getting it, feeling the rush of dopamine, and then very soon after, your dopamine crashes and you want something else to possess or experience to fill the hole inside that no object can fill.

The Native Americans have one of the most beautiful concepts in the world... or lack of concepts I should say. They have 10,000 different languages and all these tribes, and none of them have a word for ownership or possession. They don't have the concept of something from the Earth belonging to one person.

What you ultimately realize is that so much of what people get obsessed about and go crazy over is just not important. It's not necessary.

We suffer because we crave things we don't have and resent what we do have.

Most people are in a constant chase for material goods and pleasurable experiences. Some people have shopping addictions because it's become their emotional crutch. Some people, when they're feeling down, they have to go shopping. I used to be like that as a matter of fact. I used to always want the nicest clothes and the latest gadgets.

Once I realized that my apartment would have no more room for me if I keep buying things, I decided to become a minimalist.

Today, I only buy what is absolutely necessary and I think very consciously about every purchase. Before buying anything, I'll ask myself, "Do I really need this?"

Partially it's about my mental peace, partially it's about living sustainably, and part of it is bringing that higher level of consciousness to my life as I become conscious of the entire global supply chain and how my actions will affect generations to come.

Being minimalist to me doesn't mean buying the cheapest things that will break quickly and then have to be replaced, because that's actually not minimalism if you have to buy two things when you could have bought one. But minimalism does mean having only what is needed. It's the physical manifestation of psychologically letting go of the baggage we carry with us at all times.

If your mind is ever having trouble letting go of something that it is obsessing over, try letting go of some of the physical stuff you no longer need. Notice how the physical act of practicing minimalism helps create mental minimalism (inner peace).

When I gave away all of my possessions, got rid of my apartment, and decided to travel through India and Asia and South America, that's when my real experiment with minimalism began because you don't want to bring giant suitcases up and down trains, buses, and 6-story walk-up hostels. So, I only owned what I could fit in a hiking backpack.

What I found was, any more than that, you don't need it. And when you don't want it, a level of contentment, fulfillment, and deep peace comes over you.

We mistake our wants for needs all the time. When we realize we don't need much, we feel we have everything.

You may never have as much stuff as Jeff Bezos, but loving what you have makes you richer than someone who always wants more. Wanting makes us beggars in our mind.

Having been one of the poorer students at an expensive private middle school, I interacted with quite a few wealthy people.

One thing I noticed was that their tolerance for inconvenience did not exist. Rich people, I noticed, could not handle a hotel room that wasn't spotless and immaculate, with silk sheets, marble walls and gold trim. They would complain, scream, and make sure everyone knew they required the best of everything.

While that level of luxury may sound nice, I vowed never to get that way. I never wanted to lose touch with real people. I wanted to be able to go anywhere in the world and enjoy myself.

Whenever VIP concert tickets were offered to me and I could go, I always remember being amazed that people pay extra to be separated from the party and caged into a tiny corner. The majority of Americans today live greater than every king of the past, and yet we take it so for granted that we only notice how good we have it when the power goes out.

As I got older, I found that if I ever got too comfortable, it was important for me to go on a five or 10-day hiking trip with nothing but me and my backpack. That would always set me straight real quick. When all you expect is a sleeping bag and a tent, everything in life becomes a blessing. So it's about creating a constant state of gratitude so we can receive the gifts we're constantly being given.

When you have no expectations and no desire, it doesn't mean you can't have a nice house. But it does mean that you no longer blindly pursue material goods in the hope that it will bring you fulfillment, happiness, or even the envy of others.

I always thought to myself, "Why would anyone get a fancy new sports car that won't get you where you're going any better than a Honda Civic?" Only later did I realize it's not about the car. It's all about status, envy, power and ego.

For some reason, the image of Sam Walton, the billionaire founder of Walmart, driving a 20-year-old beat-up truck always struck me as the smart thing to do. Showing off seemed like the worst kind of attention to draw: from people only interested in you for your money.

Nobody has to blindly pursue material possessions. Even if you can have a rich life and have whatever you want, what really matters in life? Most people who fall for the material wealth trap are stuck in an endless pursuit for more. They end up working more, to make more, so they can waste more.

I don't know if Jeff Bezos needed to buy every mansion that he has, but I doubt he needed to buy up the whole neighborhood as well (which he did), but there's nothing wrong with that either as long as this extreme shopping isn't an addiction masking a deep unhappiness which manifests in various destructive ways in his life.

Being materially wealthy but spiritually poor is worth nothing.

When we look at what possession is, we find it's nothing more than a man-made concept and legal definition.

You can't truly own anything. Things can be near you. They can exist in a vault that exists in a house that a piece of paper says is yours and that happens to be where you spend the majority of your time. But in terms of how that affects your life, there's no difference whether you own everything or rent everything. It's no more than words on a page representing a mutually agreed fabrication.

Likewise, we don't own these bodies. We may inhabit them for a brief time, but we didn't do anything to acquire them, earn them or create them. No more can someone own the sky than own the land, these bodies, or anything else. It's not your body. It's a body and mind through which you see and operate in the world.

You become wealthy when you desire nothing. You become poor when your greed is insatiable.

Wealth, abundance, these are states of mind. If you are constantly wanting more, then you have a mentality of poverty. If you feel that everything you need you have, and everything you will need you will receive, then you are the wealthiest person there is.

So much of what people get obsessed about and go crazy over is not important at all.

The comparing mindset is one of the greatest sources of suffering on earth. It makes us fail to see the blessings we have and makes us focus solely on what someone else has that we don't have.

Until we've lived in someone else's shoes, we don't even know what they're going through. We may want someone else's life, but it may not be like their social media portrays. Comparison can turn heaven into hell. We see every day on TV, wealthy people with drama-filled lives, always competing with each other.

When we fail to identify with our infinite, eternal, miraculous true nature of bliss, joy, love and awareness; and when we misidentify with a body part or our skin color (or age, gender, name, nationality, or any other incomplete label that we often identify with), a disconnect occurs and it leads to a sense of incompleteness. A hole opens up inside us that we could spend our whole life trying to fill with stuff.

Bringing Real Happiness to Your Life

Everything we do in life is driven by an innate urge toward happiness. Whatever we think in the moment will make us the happiest, we almost always do that.

Yes, we can be disciplined and refrain from something we really want to do. And we can do something we really don't want to do.

But even then, deep down we make those decisions based on our future long term happiness. Our mind runs through a series of conscious and unconscious trade-offs, ultimately deciding what will lead to our greater happiness.

But too often, especially when we are not mindful of the future, we do things that make us happy now but miserable later. Whether it's excessive junk food, alcohol, shopping, or any other addictive behavior we partake in, we are sacrificing our future happiness for momentary pleasure.

As we incessantly chase pleasures outside of ourselves, we only succeed at creating a life that moves further and further from the true source of lasting happiness that lies within.

Many of today's problems can be traced back to a problem of affluence. One symptom of our on-demand, hyper-stimulating world is that it makes a moment of peace and quiet almost unbearable. So, we often turn to the pleasures in life to fill every moment of downtime. Whether it's pulling out our phone or always being able to count on our favorite show or movie to hypnotize us, there are so many ways to get a reliable and steady hit of dopamine. From social media to video games to workaholism to gambling, caffeine, intoxicants, and just about everything else, addiction of some kind is now, for all intents and purposes, universal.

Today because of this, relaxing and allowing some peace into our life is highly stressful. This is not a good sign for world peace anytime soon. Because we have eliminated so many of these moments of stillness in our lives, because of this excessive convenience and ubiquitous technology, we have become unfamiliar strangers with the inner peace and joy inside each of us.

Connection, empathy, compassion and love have been replaced by anonymity, envy, greed and rampant narcissism.

We have mistaken the pleasure that comes from these activities for real, lasting joy, peace and purpose. We now collectively think of a great life as one that is filled with these pleasures rather than a life filled with meaning, kindness and gratitude.

We compare and compete with people, but not in happiness; in stuff, money, and prestige.

There is nothing wrong with enjoying the pleasures of our world. But if we use them to escape ourselves and to escape this moment, then we cannot be present, we cannot heal, and we cannot fully enjoy our lives.

If we can only be happy when we are distracted and entertained, we can never be at peace. If we are using pleasure to mask some unpleasurable feelings and thoughts within us, then that is a sign we are carrying some resistance to the present moment, some lack of peace.

If we use these pleasures to suppress our unconscious rage and pain, they will only fester beneath the surface, manifesting at certain times as extreme anger, high blood pressure, a heart episode, back pain, a weakened immune system, and so many other stress and tension-related illnesses.

Wellness is like a rope. If it's pulled too tight from opposite sides, the strands will start to break until eventually the whole rope rips apart.

If we do what most successful people do and try to ignore our stress, stuff it down and power through, that stress and tension in our body will keep building up until we snap, one way or the other.

To chase life's pleasures is to choose to play a never-ending game that you cannot win.

There is no pleasure in this world that can bring lasting joy and happiness long after the activity is over. True, enduring, joyful peace can only be found within, no matter how hard we try to find it outside of us. If we are afraid to face something within, we will only run further and further from that source of infinite love and bliss at the core of who we are.

There is nothing inherently wrong with chasing pleasures your whole life, if that's what you choose to do. But real happiness will not be found outside of us, in the material world, where all things are temporary and fleeting.

What if, instead of chasing pleasures and compulsively over-consuming, over-shopping and overdoing, and instead of giving up all earthly possessions and all earthly desires, we could find and walk that middle path the Buddha talked about? What if we could tap into that infinite joy and peace within us so that we can appreciate the joys and pleasures of life when they come, and create no inner disturbance, tension, longing or craving when they leave?

In this way, we can enjoy the pleasures of the world mindfully, remain aware of their impermanence, aware of the way that their presence creates this dopamine hit, how this attachment and desire arise in the mind, and we can just witness our own cravings rather than be possessed by them.

We can notice the impulse to lose ourselves to these cravings, and we can catch ourselves before acting. We can be mindful of all aspects of the pleasures we enjoy, appreciating them without attachment, and letting go without fear.

Whenever there is possession, there is fear of loss.

If we can understand and know deeply on a subconscious level the impermanent nature of all things, then no gain nor loss can affect us. By staying connected to the permanent source of peace and joy that resides within us, then wealthy nations can enjoy what they have without fear, without attachment, without addiction, depression or anxiety.

We can consume mindfully and we can find pleasure in all the marvels of our modern society, not as a source of happiness, but as a result of our happiness.

Instead of running away from ourselves and running towards our cravings, we can appreciate the play, the dance, the drama and comedy of life.

Enjoying Things Without Letting Them Cause Any Suffering

There is a cosmic irony to this law of the universe: the

more we try, the more likely we are to fail. This law is true in sports, art, dating, earning money, and nearly everything else. The more we force effort, the more we repel the thing we want. The more pressure we put on ourselves, the more nervous we get and the more mistakes we make.

Michael Jordan worked more than anyone else. If it was forced, if he plowed through and toughed it out, he'd be tired, stressed, late and lazy, or else burn out altogether. But Jordan mastered the voice in his head, and it told him, "I love this." He did not tolerate complaints from himself and he didn't tolerate it from his teammates either, bringing out the best in everyone.

We too can always be aware of what we are thinking, swat away defeatist thoughts, and intentionally and consciously craft an unbeatable mindset.

We either control our mind, or our past will control us. The choice is up to us. All it takes is being present to break free from our conditioning.

Forced effort, no matter how hard we try, isn't sustainable. Mounting pressure does not help us perform. For some reason, the universe demands that we act without trying, achieve without striving for achievement, and get without wanting.

This is why every single expert, artist and great talent makes their job look easy. They love it so much, they've spent thousands of hours doing it for fun, and so it is easy for them.

Effort comes naturally when we're happy, peaceful and healthy because curiosity is a byproduct of being deeply present. Only when we are present can we flow through our work and the work can flow through us.

From maintaining our jobs to our families and our homes, life is constant work. Learning to enjoy it isn't just freeing; it's the only way to live up to our potential. We'll be happy to work longer, be more dedicated, committed, disciplined, creative and enthusiastic. Not as a workaholic at the office, but in working to improve every aspect of life and the life of our friends and family.

To find pleasure in the inevitable messiness of life, we have to learn to love without fear of rejection, to enjoy things without fear of loss, and to consume things without getting consumed by them.

So often the things we consume, consume us.

Our goals in life, our career, and our plans can become so important to us that they overwhelm us with fear, panic, stress and worry. If we're not careful, those emotions can turn into anger and hatred. One thing we can do is look to the great traditions of martial artists as examples. In ancient spiritual martial arts, two people may be fighting externally, but internally they maintain perfect presence, peacefulness and control. This is the epitome of external action with internal stillness — the way we can approach everything in life.

When we can peacefully witness the chaos of our mind, we bring peace to the chaos. When we watch our chaos, we create distance. When we have distance, we have freedom and power to choose wisely, act consciously, and respond intentionally.

The way martial artists achieve this balance of still action is through an ancient practice which is both spiritual and physical, learning to control their mind, to control their body, and preparing their body to react in an optimal way under stressful circumstances.

This repeated practice over and over again gets deeply rooted into the subconscious mind of the fighter, so there is no thinking that takes place during battle.

They are flowing with the present moment. There is in fact, no "fighting." They don't block powerful energetic fists or kicks, they simply redirect the energy.

If for one moment they become lost in their thoughts, they lose. If they start thinking about their next fight, they lose. If they think about the last fight or how this fight will affect their career, they lose. Even if they are consumed by the insatiable drive to win and get famous and be a huge success, instead of focusing on the present moment completely, they lose.

This is as true in martial arts as it is in the business world. In the competitive world of capitalism, while we need a goal, a vision and a plan, once those are determined and once we've set our intentions, then we need to set them aside and get to work on what needs to be done right now and give it our full attention, because the destination is not the most important thing.

The only thing that matters is the journey. If we don't put our focus on each step of the journey, we'll never reach our destination.

If we take one step that is not mindful, we can fall off a cliff. We can get completely lost if we are not paying attention. So practicing mindfulness, observing everything, and being fully present is the key to achieving our dreams.

We may even have a vision in our mind of a certain future, but if we are so attached to that outcome, we may fail to notice that it wasn't the right time and place for that business and that a new opportunity was actually 10 times better. When we're so focused on the initial plan, we become unable to adapt, we fail to see new opportunities, and we become blind to our weaknesses.

We often look at life like there's some destination to get to. But the more we realize that this is a journey — a neverending choose-your-own adventure game — the less we wait for some future outcome to bring us that moment of victorious joy.

Not one single game is about winning. They're about the quality of the experience of the game. If games were about winning, the most popular game would be a game where you just show up and everybody wins. But that would be too quick and boring.

We don't read to finish a book, we read to enjoy a book. We don't play games to win, we play because it is in our nature to be joyful.

The process is the purpose.

The process of the game of life (not to be confused with the popular board game, Life) is the fun part, the part that gives us meaning and purpose. To enjoy it is the goal, not reaching a destination, which is the same for all of us and not exactly where we're all racing to get to — that wooden box six feet under.

Yet we act like we're racing. We act like there is some finish line we're trying to get to, even though we're so afraid of that finish line that we resist thinking and talking about it. We have such a deeply rooted fear of death that it actually spurs on all other fears.

When we realize that all we're doing is racing toward our own demise, we can finally slow down and recognize that all there is this moment and all that matters is how we are experiencing this moment.

Not what is happening in the moment, but how we experience it. Are we stressed and fearful, agitated and anxious? Or are we relaxed, joyful, playful and grateful?

If life is a journey and death the destination, what good does it do to reach our destination? Our accomplishments, possessions and victories will not bring us lasting happiness. But our relationships, if we lived in wise relation to others, will provide that warmth.

If the world will end for each and every one of us, there is nothing else to do except figure out how to enjoy each moment, be as kind as possible, and make this brief experience for ourselves and everyone else as pleasant as possible. All it takes is a little bit of planning, a little bit of courage, and a little bit of practice.

With proper insight, we'll see that the greatest happiness is when the people around us are happy.

What happens when we resist putting in the work needed to reach our destination?
Ah yes, a shortcut on the journey of life. Unfortunately, it only gets us to our destination faster. We may still be alive, but if we are lazy, we are the living dead.

Sometimes, when we're following our professional dreams, we resist rolling up our sleeves, getting in there and doing the hard work that really sucks. This is very common.

If we fight against doing the essential, boring, and mundane but essential steps to building the future we're dreaming of, it usually leads to us doing one of **three things:**

1. We internalize all that stress and resistance, and then we drink our worries away at night (or engage in some other destructive coping mechanism), but that suppression of our stress only makes it accumulate until it manifests itself as chronic pain, mental illness, or some other physical condition.

2. We procrastinate and put off our goals. We stop focusing on each little moment and instead we focus on the big dream, but now it feels too big to achieve. So, we keep putting it off and putting it off because all we see is the insurmountable outcome and we're not focusing on those very little, easy and doable steps.

3. We disassociate. We are not present while we work. Mistakes get made every step of the way, building our dreams on faulty foundations riddled with cracks. And, we create a habit of mindlessly working. Mistakes that cost time and money start piling up. We can end up working longer but getting less done, or we may be making a subpar product compared to competitors who are fully focused on making the best product. Internally, this creates a strong mental habit of believing the present moment is not important, that escaping it is better, and that some future imagined time and destination will be the answer to all our problems.

The problem is, even if the day we've been working towards our whole life finally comes, because we have spent our entire life learning to resist the present moment, to keep putting off our own happiness, even when our imagined perfect life is here we'll be unable to enjoy it. We won't know how to enjoy the present, to be at peace, or to be satisfied with the rewards from our hard work.

Let's say we reach our dreams, we may still be possessed by money and the need for more. It never stops until we deal with those demons and address them, because possessions possess us.

When we have money, we fear losing it. When we have nice things, we fear their theft and so we spend money on insurance and safety deposit boxes, prison-like alarm systems and security cameras. The bigger we get, the higher the fence, the bigger the safe, and the larger security team.

Every single achievement comes with this fear and negativity attached. Money, praise, power and possessions have an insidious nature that possesses us. Society rewards us for sacrificing ourselves at the altar of money.

Of course we need to work very hard in life. It is competitive out there. But if we are attached to the results and resist the journey, our happiness will be fragile and fleeting.

It's impossible to feel deeply grateful if there is an underlying fear of loss, which stems from our desire for the temporary to be permanent.

We become so attached to things and the size of our bank account and power and fame. But all of these fleeting things are constantly changing, exchanging, coming and going. Nevertheless, we cling so hard that we become possessed. We become a possession. We will do anything to protect what we have, to keep it forever, to reclaim what we lost.

We may end up getting all the fame and wealth in the

world, but we will be possessed, manic, panicked, irrational, fearful and paranoid. Oftentimes in these states of fear and panic, we make decisions that cost us those things we're trying to hold on to and protect with our life.

This is what happens when a stock broker panics and sells everything because the market took a dip, or buys a very overvalued stock because of a fear of missing out.

Strangely enough, the greatest stock brokers are very detached. They are not emotional and they stay calm, rational and logical. The best ones do this in times of panic and they can wait out the crash and buy more again at rock bottom.

They don't ever react unconsciously to the markets; they always respond consciously with patience, perspective and wisdom. They have a set of foundational principles that guide them in times of turmoil and help them remain unshakable.

This is a metaphor for life because most of the time we are unconsciously reacting. We are not mindful of ourselves, our situations, or our mental state. We are nearly always lost in thought, fearful and stressed, and reacting impulsively instead of acting intentionally.

Underlying stress is fear. When fearful thinking takes over, whether it's in business or in personal relationships, we lose our mindful awareness, our presence of attention, and our sense of agency and autonomy.

The possession completely grabs hold of us. We go into our conditioned, habitual, auto pilot mode. The preloaded software in our brain takes us over and we become possessed by whatever is our primary driver, whether it's work and earning money, finding love, or having the right house in the right neighborhood so kids can go to the right school. All sources of stress, which at its core is fear.

Not only in the martial arts, but in love too, if we are stressed, fearful and panicked, or if we are obsessed, desperate and needy, we will push people and our dreams away. When we are present, confident, thoughtful and in control, we become much more attractive and capable.

Isn't it strange that neediness is repulsive to the universe? Everything is ours when we act like we don't even want it. Perhaps because the universe put everything here for us to enjoy and appreciate, and neediness implies we have forgotten our infinite blessings.

Whether it's making money, dating, or achieving any other type of goal, as they say in the movie, Super Troopers, "Desperation is a stinky cologne."

A potential customer can smell the desperation of a salesman and easily say, "No." A potential romantic partner often wants to be with someone who believes in themselves, not someone who comes off as needy.

If a martial artist has one moment of doubt, if they feel insecure, worried and scared, or they feel rushed or off-balance, then it's game over. These are the same emotions that sweep us away when it comes to money, love, sports, academic pursuits and personal achievement.

The way to not get swept away is to stay present, to stay mindful, and not get swept away by these heavy emotions we have around those things we've been working our whole life towards and building up so much in our mind.

Losing ourselves means that we've lost our presence, we've lost awareness of ourselves. The true "I", our highest wisdom and intelligence, our conscious awareness that determines where we put our focus and attention and energy, disappears from our perception. We lose these greater mental faculties as we become unaware. We go from eternal souls to preprogrammed automatons. **We are lost in thought instead of witnessing thought.**

It is in these lost moments, when the commanding generals in our brain are out to lunch, that we allow for other things to possess us, to fill in for that vacancy and assume that role when our better judgment and capabilities are gone.

This is when we are not careful and when we are at the whim of other people, other things, other circumstances and situations. This is when we become overwhelmed with emotion, worry and insecurity.

So just like the martial artist, we have to apply a practice to address those things that cause us to lose ourselves. We do that simply by thinking deeply about what disturbs us or whatever problem we need to solve.

For example in meditation, once we reach a relaxed state we can then meditate on money. We can meditate on our intentions, our goals, our plans and our greatest hopes. We can recognize and analyze how much is enough, what cost are we willing to bear, what are we willing to sacrifice, and what do we want our day-to-day life to look like. This may look different for every one of us.

Each one of us has within our heart the greatest source of knowing and intuition for what we need to do in each moment.

Like every single animal on Earth, and who have far smaller brains than us yet live out equally complex lives, we too have everything we need, all of the answers, inside of us.

So every day, we can do this. This is called **analytical**

meditation.

We can start the meditation by focusing on our breath or a mantra (Om will do fine) for a few minutes.

Then, once we reach that highly relaxed state that hypnotists operate in — where we become very suggestible and able to access deep into our subconscious mind — we get to work on our problems.

We use this clearer thinking to focus on things like where we want to be in five years, and what we need to do today to achieve that.

It's important to set clear goals and intentions, and then focus on what needs to be done in this moment only.

That is all that matters because the key to a happy life is having our intentions, goals and actions in full alignment. Action stems from our thoughts which stem from our intentions underneath.

Most people don't spend time reflecting on who they are, what their core values are, what really matters to them and what they really want in life.

It's hard to see what we'll want in the future. Young people don't usually fear dying alone, but by the time the fear sets in, they're already old and alone while their peers have spent decades building families. We may think we want money and fame when we're young, but we may long for a simple life when we're older.

The beauty is, there are no mistakes. Only play, exploration and discovery. And as long as we keep moving forward and never quit, we can always change our mind. It's only when we get stuck, paralyzed by fear, and unable to make that change that we start to live out of alignment.

When we are fully aligned, there is no internal conflict. When we expect and even embrace difficulties, hardships and challenges, then we no longer get swept away by them.

Then nothing can take control of us because there is no vacancy inside of us that needs filling. We are complete, we are whole, and we are present.

We can let go of our attachment to future outcomes because we know that if we do what we need to do in this moment, with our fullest attention and awareness, the future will take care of itself.

The future is created in the now. If we fixate on the future, we develop fear, insecurity, stress and anxiety.

We may have enough to survive today, but what about tomorrow? While being aware of life's uncertainty can motivate us to work harder, to focus more on the people in our lives, and to be more grateful; if we fear the uncertain future, we open the door to becoming possessed by our fear.

Financial possession takes hold because there's never an amount of money that is truly satisfying. If we have money today, we can fear we may lose it tomorrow.

Fame, money and success are fleeting. If we worship at their altar, if we expect them to be our salvation, we will be sorely disappointed. Just ask a younger Jim Carrey, Matthew Perry, or any other member of the Depressed Rich and Famous Club.

When we attach to something temporary, we are setting ourselves up for future suffering because nothing lasts forever. Ups and downs, cycles and constant change are the fundamental laws of this material universe now. Instead of resisting change, we can embrace the fleeting beauty of life.

It is impermanence that makes a flower's brief bloom so precious. We appreciate the rare and fleeting, and we take for granted that which we expect to always be there for us. The more we understand impermanence, the more we can simply appreciate and welcome each moment as it comes.

Knowing that everything is fleeting doesn't mean we become careless, leave our doors unlocked, not wear seatbelts, or spend money like there's no tomorrow. If we appreciate something, we care for it and protect it without that insecure, grasping, need to possess it. We can still get an alarm system if we need one. We won't keep all our money on the front lawn and just hope for the best.

We still plan, we still have a vision for the future, and we still try to create some sense of security and safety; but we do it with presence and conscientiousness, a focus on the now, and a trust that by caring for this moment the future will take care of itself.

When our hopes for the future turn into a source of fear and suffering, then a detrimental attachment has developed. Nonattachment is the key to achieving without striving.

Martial artists and elite athletes, even successful entrepreneurs, will employ the powerful practice of visualization to help them be present, prepared, and unattached.

By visualizing an experience in your mind, the same neural activity takes place in the brain as if you were actually having the real experience. If you visualize eating a cake, your mind will think it's eating cake. And so athletes and martial artists will visualize an entire game or an entire fight in their head, and they will visualize themselves performing at their optimum peak level and winning. This creates muscle memory in the body and mind so that they can react quicker than the speed of thought, and it creates confidence, courage and calm.

Buddhist monks also use visualizations. For example, their meditation on death involves visualizing everyone they know and love growing old and dying. They will see it all happening before their mind's eye, everyone aging and decaying, including themselves. Some monks will even do this inside morgues beside the bodies in order to fully immerse themselves in this visualization.

Now, we don't have to go to such an extreme example. What we can all do is, when we get a new car, we can meditate on its demise. We can visualize it getting scratched, stolen, vandalized, breaking down... All of the worst fears that we may have about it, we can visualize.

Then, we visualize ourselves responding to the situation with calm, strength and wisdom. We see ourselves react exactly how we would wish if we were most mindful of ourselves.

We do this over and over again until our wise, conscious response becomes more ingrained in our psyche than our unconscious, unwise, automatic reaction.

We can do this visualization practice to alleviate all of our fears, whether it's losing a job, losing all our money in a stock market crash, or public speaking. **By preparing for panic we can avoid panic.**

If we are working on losing weight, quitting an addiction, becoming more disciplined, a better athlete, or anything else, visualization can help us create new habits and behaviors. Through repeated visualization, we can gain valuable experience and insight, create new neural pathways in the brain (which is responsible for forging new habits and skills), and it can help us achieve goals, quit harmful behavior, and come to terms with loss, disrepute, and grief.

While it seems counterintuitive to visualize what we don't want, what this is doing is freeing us from the fear by facing it before it happens. Then, our biggest fears not only are less likely to happen because we are operating from a more relaxed, more confident, more stress-free state; but even if our fear does come true, we are not going to suffer because we knew it could happen, we anticipated it, we mentally prepared and practiced for it, and so we know how to respond to it.

Visualization is one of the most profound practices for facing our fears and attachments, for letting go of the things we cling to, and for achieving without striving. It's how we can stay grounded and not get swept away by greed, praise or criticism. It's how we can stay true to ourselves, reach our dreams, enjoy the journey, inhabit the traits we wish to have, create a mindset for success, and be prepared for success so that when it comes we know how to keep it.

Life Lesson 6

Bad and Good Are One.
Thinking Makes It Two.

When you can step back and see the big picture, and know that good things will come, good things will go, bad things will come, and bad things will go, then your happiness doesn't rely on any kind of external situation. That's the key to lasting happiness.

Life's about enjoying the good times while they're here and knowing they won't last. And when the bad times come, we know they won't last either.

How we approach the ups and downs of life tells us how we view our own ever-changing reality, which can be done in one of three ways.

1) Optimistically
2) Pessimistically
3) Seeing things as they truly are (notice I don't say "realistic," because no one can predict the future accurately).

Optimism is delusional. Pessimism is negative and delusional. But to see things as they truly are is to awe at the beauty of the universe rather than some imagined version in your head.

To see things as they truly are without resistance, hate, anger or jealousy brings about a deep peace and inner calm. It is to live in alignment with everything that is happening in the universe, to understand ourselves, others, and even what is unknowable, without projecting our own subjective and limited interpretation.

The only healthy way to deal with the ups and downs of life is to welcome them both equally. We can allow for the ups and downs to be our teachers, to be the training grounds for our mind. Life will contain all the joys and sorrow. But sorrow gives way to joy and joy to sorrow. Violent times lead to peaceful times and peaceful times lead to violence. Will we be surprised by any of it, or will we be a source of strength for ourselves, our loved ones, and our communities?

As hard as we try, no one escapes sickness and death. It will happen to everyone we know and love. But these natural processes, these cycles of change, these continuations of transformation from form to energy and energy to form, are beautiful and essential to life living on. All the joy that comes from the birth of a newborn is even contained within that child's later sicknesses and eventual death, because they cannot be separated from the entirety of the process of life on this planet.

If life could live forever, there would be no evolution because there would be no survival of the fittest. We are only here because of the journey of our ancestors, not just in your family, but our species and life as a whole. Every single bad moment in life has led to every single moment of bliss. Life clears away the old to make way for something better.

Whatever the situation we're facing in our lives, good or bad, financial or medical, whether it's the best news or the worst news, we can simply be that witnessing presence, witnessing our emotions, and witnessing our thoughts. In good times, we can mindfully make sure we don't become arrogant, unappreciative, or attached to success and praise. In bad times, we can mindfully observe our tendencies toward fear, anger and avoidance.

Hard times are great times.

I know, I know. You're thinking I must've gone mad. And you'd be correct if you thought I meant we should try to create hard times. What I really mean is, there is value to every single challenging moment in our lives. No matter how senseless a tragedy we face in our lives, we have the opportunity to learn how to heal and how to help heal others.

Hard times keep us grounded, empathic, and connected to the suffering of our fellow man. They lead us toward the path of peace, healing, compassion and reconciliation. Only when we understand suffering can we help others in need.

Be extra careful in good times.

When I was in my twenties working at a big ad agency in New York, one of my coworkers got a big promotion and decided to go out that night to celebrate.

He began the night at a bar after work with some coworkers. He then went back to his apartment with a few friends while they waited for his girlfriend to get home before going out for more partying. While drinking and smoking on his fire escape, he fell over the railing and tragically did not survive the fall.

This is something that could have happened to me any of the number of times I was hanging out on a fire escape, like we all do, drinking and having fun, but flying a little too close to the sun.

To be totally honest, I passed out once on a fire escape in New York City and I was lucky that I didn't fall in the wrong direction.

Like my former coworker, I too was overstressed, overworked, and had no idea what to do about it.

Thankfully, my suffering led me to find these ancient teachings that I am now able to share with the world, and in the memory of those beautiful souls we lost too soon.

It is precisely by loving our hard times and staying mindful during challenging times that we can bring in some presence, clarity and stillness to every moment. When we can remain in that state of inner joy which comes from a deep and unshakable peace.

We can remain equanimous no matter what, no situation can disturb our inner peace, and we can become that radiating center of peace for ourselves and others.

In this state, whatever comes into our field of awareness gets transformed by our peaceful, radiating energy.

The same way we are affected by the energy other people carry with them, when we tap into that peace within us, it creates a powerful ripple effect all around us. Through either meditation, mindfulness, yoga, art, or anything else that pulls us into the present moment, a nonthinking peaceful energy of calm serenity and spaciousness is created that deeply heals and affects those around us.

It is these grounding, recentering activities which root us firmly in the present moment and enable us to endure, survive and thrive no matter what life throws our way. Life either pushes us over, or we push back. Like a martial artist, with inner strength and balance, nothing can keep us down.

Sailing Through the Ups and Downs of Life

When I meditated for the first time, a rush of thoughts came over me the whole time, mostly negative. I could not sit still for more than 30 seconds. I wanted to scratch my head, my nose, my eyes out. I kept saying how much I hated it in my mind, and, "This sucks!"

I was constantly fidgeting, couldn't keep my eyes closed for more than a minute, and didn't see the point. "Why does anybody do this?" I thought. And I was pretty sure that the other meditators and the instructor were crazy.

But afterwards, even though in this hour-long class I felt like I had probably meditated properly for a total of only two seconds, I still felt a greater peace afterward than I had ever known.

It was like going to a friend or therapist, dumping all my complaints on them, and then getting too exhausted to complain about anything for at least the next 24 hours.

Now, I knew that meditation wasn't magic and that I hadn't become enlightened overnight. I knew that if I had spent 200,000 hours of my life, or however long I've been alive, not meditating, to suddenly try to be in this totally different state of being would not be easy or natural. I wouldn't pick up a guitar for the first time and expect to play like Jimi Hendrix.

Meditation is like any other skill. Learning a new language or an instrument takes a little while, but you can still get joy out of it right away. And, you can still enjoy the process.

But when you've spent your whole life not playing the guitar, playing the guitar is gonna feel strange and difficult at first. You may even think to yourself, "Guitar isn't for me! Maybe other people are born with the gift, but not me."

But if you stick to that new skill, even if you feel like you're not making any progress, one day it can suddenly "click," and you'll be blown away by how far you've come. You may not be an expert yet or the world's best, but the journey of growth is the same.

When we partake in activities that pay off over time, our happiness grows and grows. When we partake in an activity that gives us instant reward for little effort, our happiness declines over time.

And there is **no activity that contributes to our long term happiness more than meditation because meditation improves every other activity we do.**

When I first started meditating, it took me a pretty long time before I got the hang of it and developed a consistent practice. After two or three months of consistency though, it finally became very clear that meditation had completely transformed my life for the better.

Then, a few months later during a particularly chaotic time in my life, my meditation practice made a U-turn. It was like I had forgotten how to meditate. I was so easily distracted that as soon as I sat down and closed my eyes, my mind had already run off. I would even forget that I was meditating while I was meditating! My mind was constantly racing in my meditations for a few months, until I realized my obstacle: I was comparing my current meditation to my great ones in the past. Because of this, I was unable to learn what my mind was trying to show me, and I was resisting and fighting against the natural ups and downs of life.

One of the biggest obstacles to meditation is expectations.

It never goes the way we expect. Of course we want it to be dreamy and easy, but sometimes our mind needs to face its own dark corners. The best thing is to let go of all expectations.

One time you might have an incredible experience. Then the next time may be a normal experience, but that will cause enormous frustration because now we expected an even better meditation than the last one, which suddenly makes this normal one seem like a disappointment.

The whole point of meditation is to simply allow for whatever comes into our field of awareness. To observe the good, the bad, and the neutral all the same. Notice how experience is constantly changing, without judgment, and with a peaceful equanimity.

Sometimes you'll start meditating and you'll have an incredible experience right from the beginning. Then, maybe, the next time's not so good. Maybe it stays not so good for a long time. That's okay. It's not about seeing fireworks and having a nirvanic experience. It's about how it changes the rest of your life.

Meditation is not about meditation. Meditation is about how you interact with the world outside of meditation.

It's important to not lose focus on your intention behind your meditation practice. If you get caught up in the meditation itself, it can be disappointing. But if you remember why you're meditating — whether it's for reaching your greatest potential, for being more present with your family and friends, for the benefit of all living beings, for better focus and discipline, for more peace and happiness, or for all of the above — then you can let go of expectations, relax into your practice, and sustain your practice through difficult times.

Handling Bad Times in Life

Every human being has an innate urge, and a human right, to experience all of the things that make life so meaningful — friendship, family, freedom, art, poetry, music, and nature. Spirituality is no replacement for any of these things, just like how no amount of meditation will fill our bellies with food. But when relationships inevitably end, when there is global unrest, when nature is going through its endless cycle of death and rebirth, **spirituality can help us see the deeper eternal truth beyond the fleeting change of forms.**

But what can we do when things in our life are very bad, when being present is the last place we want to be? What spiritual balms are there for those extremely hard phases of life, like when we're confronted with our own impending mortality, or when we witness the death of a loved one?

A lot of people think that "being present" during a difficult time means to suffer in that difficult moment.

But no matter how hard we try to run away from the present moment or ourselves, we will never escape. So actually, being present means realizing that the way out of our suffering is through the here and now.

When difficult times come, such as grief, it's not the present moment that is insufferable; it's the loss that occurred in our past, which we are unconsciously and unintentionally bringing into the present moment.

To dwell on our loss is to cling onto the past. If we try to run away from our suffering, it will follow us everywhere we go. The only thing we can do is sit with our present moment suffering.

To sit is to witness, to hold space, to allow and care for our hurt bodies and souls. It is to realize that in the present moment, when we're fully present, fully alert and aware, free from the cloud of thought and judgment, that there are no problems. There are only temporary physical forms constantly changing all around us.

Good times, bad times — these are judgments we make that color our experiences as good or bad. I'm not suggesting that you won't feel sad or stressed in certain times, but the quickest way out of it is to do the thing we're avoiding, that we want to look away from, that we're afraid of.

The best thing to do is…
Turn and face the monster in our life, that thing we're too afraid to look at. Only then will you realize that no matter how difficult of a time you're going

through, it's OK, this too will change, and the universe will keep on unfolding in perfect harmony and balance.

The urge we have to avoid our pain, drink ourselves numb, and distract ourselves with work or entertainment, only makes the situation worse. These things make us unhealthy, stress the body and mind, and cloud our thinking and judgment. They make the path back to health and happiness much harder and longer. If we can look at our pain and sit with it, we'll notice it's not as unbearable as we think it will be. It's nothing more than thoughts — words in our head — and the harmless subtle sensations in the body.

Sometimes Life Throws Us Challenges

Every single one of us will face challenging times in our lives. There is no escaping it. We sure try though. We focus on work, escape with drinks, stuff down feelings with food, become engrossed in entertainment, or take on some other form of avoidance. All until we've decided enough is enough and it's time to be present with what we're experiencing.

When we're present, and not running away, the healing can begin. In the present moment, along with whatever we're feeling or facing, there is also peace. In that peace, we will find strength.

We all have an inner light of peace radiating within us — our true nature. Sometimes the world can diminish it, but it cannot put that light out.

When we become present, we strengthen, brighten and expand that light. Presence is like dumping gasoline on that peace pilot light. It can completely engulf us and we can remain at peace no matter what's going on around us. This peaceful energy will be felt around you by others and will create countless positive ripple effects wherever you go.

So many times throughout our lives, whenever we're going through difficult times, we wonder, "How am I going to get through this?" We're always wondering how our future is going to be. We don't think we'll be able to survive the scary future. We think the past was so bad that it must mean that our future is ruined. And so we feel the dreadful sensation of looming and impending doom.

But here's the thing, we've always gotten through everything we've ever faced. We may feel like failures and losers, but we are survivors, fighters, and winners.

The way through difficult times isn't in the past, and it isn't in the future. It's in this moment.

It'll get tough. It'll be hard. And you'll take each moment as it comes, not holding onto the last moment, not afraid of the next one, and you'll let go of this one with ease as you welcome the next one with peace and gratitude. You'll know what each moment requires of you in the moment. The moment is where all the answers present themselves.

When we're moving and flowing with the present moment, responding to whatever comes up with intention and consciousness, we're mindful of our thoughts and feelings.

We'll listen to our body and give it what it needs, whether that's exercise or rest or even having a good cry.

When we take the weight of our past and future onto our shoulders at all times, it is too grinding and we're unable to stand up and face our challenging times.

But when we are fully in the moment, leaving the past in the past and the future in the future, we can handle any moment. With total awareness and presence, we can express ourselves when needed, take action when the moment calls for it, and remain at peace when stillness is required.

Becoming present is as simple as noticing your own awareness and focus. Usually, we focus on the things we're focusing on.

But to be blasted into the peaceful present moment, to expand our consciousness, we have to become conscious of our own consciousness.

Notice yourself noticing. This is what being present and fully aware is all about. Make it a regular practice to notice where your attention is, what you are thinking, and how you are feeling over every part of your body. Notice your emotions and any tension or stress you may be holding on to.

As you look at yourself looking around, practice looking without labeling. Don't skip over an object because you've seen it a million times.

Really look at everything you're looking at. Really listen without labeling all the sounds that you hear. The more we make being present a habit, the more we can handle any challenge with peace, calm and clarity.

We will all face challenging times in our lives no matter who we are. It doesn't matter if we're super wealthy or super in debt.

And the funny thing about human psychology is that we have a wide range of pain tolerance that is different for every single person based on their past and their biology.

For example, if two people are given a number scale and told 1 is equal to no pain and 10 is equal to the most pain imaginable, a shock of 400 volts of electricity may hurt like a 10 to one person. But maybe the other person is a big tough football player and is used to pain. They might say it only felt like a 2. But, if the football player happened to be depressed that day, that could change their answer to 10.

So what is painful to one person can be painless to someone else. To one person, pain could be worrying about how to pay the bills. To another person, it may be seeing someone else wearing the same exact dress at a fancy event.

Everyone's hardest 10-level of pain moment is equal to everyone else's, even though the stories and magnitude may be completely different.

And while we cannot escape challenging times, we can free ourselves from the pain that they cause. By understanding this Theory of Pain Relativity, we can step out of our mental story about the pain, we can see it from a broader perspective, we can create some distance, and we can watch it with peacefulness.

Like dentists who are now offering Pain Meditation as an alternative to pain medication have discovered, we can all change our perception of pain. We can all become masters of our mind.

If we can remain present through difficult times, if there is no weight on our shoulders from the past or the future, if we are aware of our thoughts and not lost in them, then we can get through anything.

Making Peace With Change

When we do something over and over again, our brains no longer have to think about it. We do it automatically. It's like we are taken over by an automatic impulse. We can completely lose ourselves in a repeated activity. Because we no longer have to be present, we don't have to think about every step of what we're doing. It's what athletes call muscle memory and what scientists call strongly developed neural pathways in the brain. This is the human body running on autopilot.

This neuroplasticity that allows us to form new habits is why we can take a shower in the morning, eat breakfast, and even drive to work, and yet have no memory of these things taking place.

That's because we were zoned out the whole time, barely conscious of what was happening. We can be looking over our shoulder when backing out of the driveway, checking our mirrors before changing lanes, but do it all completely automatically, as if we're out of our body. Anything we've been doing for a long time can become second nature, for better and worse.

So the brain, which does this in order to save brainpower and maximize efficiency, creates these automatic series of actions so that we can be alert to our surroundings while we're doing something mundane.

The problem is, when we're engaged in a task for the purpose of escape, then over time our futile attempt to escape our own mind ends up enslaving us.

Eventually, we start compulsively accumulating bad habits. We become attached to familiar pleasures and people, whether they're good for us or not. We even become attached to our identity and a contrived personality. We identify with ways of thinking and ways of believing.

Often we become attached to our very own mindset of attachment. Here we crave certain luxuries or we crave certain experiences, or we are attached to having a certain social life or a romantic partner. So when we experience our situations change, and our attachment is no longer there, then we suffer immensely.

When something we have become so accustomed to is no longer in our lives, it terrifies the ego because it found safety in that attachment. It thought it knew what was going to happen, it thought there was predictability and safety, and then its expectations were shattered. Now, according to the brain, it's in danger.

This is why our brains crave repetition, seek out stability, and become accustomed to whatever is familiar. While this is beneficial for survival, it is easy to see how this mindset can become a hindrance in modern society; how it can lead to fear, even fear of leaving the house, fear of trying new things or changing careers. It can prevent us from leaving an abusive partner too.

Many people live in a constant state of subtle, unnoticeable discontent stemming from our attachment to comparing ourselves with others. We'll endlessly chase after material possessions, be fearful that we won't have enough, won't have more than the next guy, or that we could lose our precious stuff. The natural processes of the brain that served humans well for hundreds of thousands of years, have been hijacked by advertisements, mass production, technology, and unnatural foods and substances. The craving, yearning, exploring human spirit was diverted and channeled into apps and brands.

Now we crave such specific things, specific experiences, specific luxuries and pleasures, that it completely consumes us. **Things that didn't exist a few decades ago, we act like we could never live without.**

We are always fearful of losing what we have, ungrateful for what we do have, and afraid of change. That is the essence of attachment when you get right down to it — misidentifying temporary phenomena as permanent. Stability, consistency and permanence do not exist.

The only thing that is unchanging and permanent is no thing, empty space. All matter, all energy and all mental activity are constantly changing.

Just as empty space is the place from which all matter and energy emerge, within each one of us there is a blank canvas in the back of our minds.

All of our sense perceptions — the sights, sounds, smells and tastes we experience — are projected onto that blank canvas, that inner spaciousness through which our perception of experience emerges. That is our true unchanging Self.

When we fail to identify with that non-material consciousness inside of us, that essence of who we are beneath the aging body and brain, then we begin to feel like fleeting, temporary, aging bodies. We'll grasp at anything we can attach ourselves to, anything that seems stable, in order to not feel the dreadful fleeting nature of our existence. And so, we cling to the illusion of permanence and stability.

We'll grab hold of anything we can — religion, the "old ways," our loved ones, our success — even though everything is changing constantly and rapidly. We'll risk everything on this quest for security. We lose ourselves trying not to lose ourselves.

On a conscious level, we know that everybody is aging, that everybody is growing old and is going to die, that all the stuff around us is deteriorating and decomposing, and that in a 100 years or 1000 years it will all dissolve into dust. But because we don't see that change happening in front of our eyes, because the change is too slow to perceive, we become taken in by the illusion of permanence.

We believe that there can be some peace and comfort if we cling tight enough to the illusion. We think we can have stability and that we won't have to fear a changing future. This delusion, which is the first attachment that we develop and that all attachments stem from, is the cause of nearly all suffering.

We think a stable life will create a peaceful mind, but a peaceful mind creates a stable life.

Most of the time, attachment and craving push away the people and things we want to attract. For example, we could be driving a very expensive car. If we are so worried and cautious that we only drive it five miles an hour, even on the highway, we could cause a terrible crash.

Fear makes us more likely to make mistakes, not less. And underlying all fear is attachment.

Attachment to our identity, to success, and to praise and prestige is why talking on a stage to 1,000 people feels harder than speaking to one person in private. Unless that person is interviewing us for a job or a loan, in which case our attachment to a desired outcome rears its ugly head again.

The more we are attached to any outcome, whether it's doing good works or achieving success, the more pressure we put on ourselves. We'll be more nervous and we are going to perform much worse. When we are totally in our head, lost in thought and worry, we cannot respond to the present moment with confidence, clarity and calm.

If we really really really want a romantic partner, we'll

overthink everything, come off as insecure, and fail to connect. If we're too attached to success, we're more likely to make costly mistakes or take shortcuts.

So this is that catch-22 of manifesting, which is when we cling to a person, we come off as needy. When we cling to a goal, we come off as too eager and unready. **Attachment repels, detachment attracts.**

When we are detached and we are thinking clearly, we are much more likely to attract all of the blessings of this world. We are more likely to project confidence and ease, and more likely to get the things we want. When we stop wanting it so much, we get it. That's because not wanting projects the energy that we could have anything anytime we want and it's no big deal.

When we are attached to a person or thing, that person or thing controls us. When we let go of attachment, that thing or person is more likely to come into our lives because we are in control. Being in control, being free from desires, attachments, and clinging, is attractive. And it even gets rewarded in business.

People are more likely to follow leaders who appear as though they have no desire to control or manipulate people. All animals can sense when people are comfortable in their own skin and at peace, or fearful that things may or may not work out.

So, to achieve everything we want in life, without attachment, is to act externally with stillness internally.

That is what it means to be in a flow state, to be fully present with your full attention on your fingertips while you're doing something, closely observing and truly seeing whatever you're looking at.

When we are fully present, no thoughts have room to come in because as soon as thoughts come in, we're lost in thought and we're not paying attention to what's right in front of us. A distracted mind lost in thought is always clinging, grasping, and attaching to mental constructs of its own making. We become like a hamster running in a hamster wheel, going nowhere while wasting tremendous energy, unable to get off.

The main cause of boredom is a distracted mind.

Boredom is the feeling of loss that stems from constantly comparing this moment to the past. Every moment that passes is another moment lost to us. Our mind goes into a tailspin, thinking of the better things we could be doing, thinking of the things we'd like to scream, but the one thing we cannot do is focus on the present moment.

When the mind is at rest, we can do laborious tasks with ease. When we feel like we're sprinting on a hamster wheel, the slightest inconvenience can make us explode. And it all has to do with whether our mind is still, our focus unwavering, and our attention unshakable.

To break free from this attachment to thinking, we need to do **two things**:

1. First, we have to lengthen our focus, increase our attention, and expand our awareness.

   When we can control our focus, we are no longer a victim of our thoughts. We create them. We no longer get taken away by thoughts. We become free from them. We no longer waste time thinking about tomorrow or yesterday. We give people and places the full and undivided attention they deserve. We are fully invested in this peaceful present moment, and it is always peaceful, even when the world around us is chaotic, if our minds are peaceful.

The universe does not exist outside of us. Every living being experiences a mental simulation of the universe around them from inside their own mind. **By thinking, "Things are so chaotic!" we create all of the chaos we experience.**

There is no real chaos in the world. It is only the interpretation of a scared brain that is working overtime to make us suffer. If we expect peace, chaos will be upsetting. **If we expect peace and chaos, we can remain at peace through both.** If our mind is always jumping around wildly like a kangaroo on a trampoline, even peace will appear chaotic. But by increasing our ability to focus, we can increase the peace in our life immeasurably.

2. Once we can direct our attention, we're then able to shift it to the present moment.

The good news is, meditation is both the practice of directed/guided/intentional focus, and present moment awareness. So through meditation, peace becomes our natural state of being. Meditation provides the base, mindfulness becomes the habit, and then life can flow through us effortlessly, like it does through every other plant and animal.

Because in meditation we are focusing on something in this moment — either the breath, the body, a mantra or a guided meditation — we are always focusing on the present moment. We're not focusing on the last breath, the last mantra, how our body felt 10 minutes ago, or the next instruction in the guided meditation. We simply practice staying in this moment.

By practicing focusing on this moment, we increase our presence. We begin to move beyond thought, attachment and clingingness. We develop our mental muscle for focus, a habit of being present, and we incidentally develop a greater capacity to focus on whatever else we want to improve in our lives — music, art, our business, our health…

As we begin to practice, the mind stops constantly jumping around like a monkey, swinging from thought to thought aimlessly. We become the captain of our reality, destiny, inner universe, and how we relate to the universe around us. As the still witnessing presence of consciousness, we recognize the impermanent, constantly changing, illusory existence all around us.

Because we witness the change, we are not the change.

The more we practice, the more we become comfortable letting things come and go. Our new habit of mind becomes compassionate detachment, and ultimately, free from the suffering of change, aging and loss.

Life Lesson 7

Happiness and Success
Are Not the Same

A lot of people in our modern materialistic world think that success equals happiness and that if they get this position or that raise or a big bonus, they'll finally be happy. But personal experience, as well as scientific studies, have shown that once people's basic needs are met, more money, more success, and bigger titles do not make us happy. If we believe success will be the key to our happiness, there will never be enough to satisfy us, we'll obsess about what others have that we don't, and we'll fail to see and appreciate the blessings we already have.

When a person gets a big raise or promotion, they'll get a big rush of dopamine, and then it very quickly wears off. Within a couple days we're back to being the exact same as before — stressed, worried, insecure and restless.

There are a lot of people who sell success as the key to happiness. Everyday, our society says, "Don't worry about happiness now. You can do that once you've made it." **And so people go their whole life waiting to be happy, only to find that happiness is not in their bank account.** It's not in their job title. They'll miss their kids growing up, they'll forget what their spouse looks like, and they'll let stress and illness eat at them, all while searching for the wrong goal in life.

Whoever is the happiest is the richest.

Happy people don't think, "If only I had this or that, my life would be complete." They feel complete already.

Many people who come to India notice how so many poor and homeless people look so happy with big smiles on their faces. It's often a shock to go back to the U.S. and see wealthy people who are struggling severely, whose families don't talk to each other, and who don't know their neighbors' names.

Chasing superficial goals can only bring superficial results. They may look happy on the surface, but money won't hug you back. **Real happiness is in our mindset, in our relationships, and in the quality of our thoughts and emotions.**

It's okay to want nice things and have big goals, as long as it's done from a place of joy, where you can enjoy the journey regardless of the outcome so that no matter what happens, you can look back and feel good about your life.

Happiness can even come from failure.

It is not uncommon for spiritual awakenings to happen on the worst day of a person's life. Their ego is able to die because they have suffered so much that all of a sudden, out of self-preservation, the mind wakes up out of the dream world and out of the delusion of past and future. When all is darkest and we feel that we can take no more, suddenly in an instant, everything changes.

Happiness is More Than Success
So much of human suffering is caused by mistaking wants for needs.

Once our needs are met — a roof over our heads, food, clothes, job, security, health — that's when our needless suffering begins, because now we want MORE. We compete for more, we are jealous of others who have more, and we feel we *need* more instead of *wanting* more.

Despite what is portrayed in the media, happiness is not determined by the numbers on our bank statements. Happiness is based on how much peace, love, gratitude, and compassion we have within us.

Our true happiness can be measured by how we feel when all our gadgets and gizmos are put down at the end of the night, when we close our eyes to go to sleep and are left with nothing but ourselves and our thoughts.

Whether we have high-powered stressful jobs, or whether we are stressed about not having enough money, our happiness depends on how we view these stressful situations.

Situations can be stressful, but we do not have to internalize the stress. We can either flow with whatever is happening, or we can resist it. The choice is ours. In every single moment, we have this choice.

We cannot buy our way out of stress.

But by turning inward and tapping into the peace and joy we all have within us, we can release our stress and find the joy that is always right here, right now.

Most people believe that success leads to happiness. We look up to people who are more successful than us with jealousy, and it creates immense suffering in our lives. But financial success is not related to happiness.

Jim Carrey famously talks about how he was never happy growing up. He thought if he had some success, he could finally be happy. Then, he became more successful than he ever dreamed. He had more fame and money than he ever thought possible. And yet, he was still unhappy. He was still in the exact same mental place as before his success.

It's normal in our society to think that we should put off our happiness until we've achieved success, and only then can we be happy. But we have to learn to be happy now, even while struggling and scraping by. **Because there is only now.**

What we do with this moment, and how we treat ourselves in this moment, determines how we'll feel in future moments.

The goal of life is happiness. Happiness drives every choice we make. We'll even make ourselves miserable to try and be happy, like working 80-hour weeks or living in places we don't like.

Don't get me wrong, we often need to make sacrifices for the things we need in life. We do need some measure of material and financial achievement to survive. Misery occurs when we confuse needs for wants.

We think if we get the things we want that we'll be happy. But once we can finally put food on the table, a roof over our head, afford transportation, access health care and have all our basic needs met, more money has no impact on our happiness.

How many times have we said, "I *need* a new (fill in the blank)," when truthfully we *wanted* one? All the time, right? The language we use when speaking to ourself matters.

So we have to ask ourselves, "Is my language reminding myself that the universe always provides? Or is it reminding me that there is a scarcity of opportunity and resources?"

Needs are necessary and important. Wants are based on a mental attachment to what is perceived as pleasant. Wants can be both conditioned and innate, and wants can be changed both intentionally and unintentionally.

Wants and needs can both be experienced peacefully and mindfully, but trillions of dollars are spent every year to make us confuse wants for needs.

Ads tell us that wants are good, and we should indulge. That we need to work harder so we can finally "arrive," whatever that means. I guess if our mind is always lost, it'd be nice to finally arrive.

It's wonderful to strive for achievements. We want to look back on our lives and see that we worked hard and achieved great things. So the question becomes, can we enjoy the journey? Can we create some space, peace and stillness in the striving? Can we see the ups and downs of our journey with a broader perspective so that we don't lose ourselves along the way, so we don't stress out over every temporary setback, and so we don't become cocky or arrogant in our up moments? Can we maintain equanimity, calm and clarity no matter what is happening around us? The answer is yes.

We all have the ability within us to center ourselves. Every second we are breathing, we have the ability to breathe out any tension and stress we're holding onto.

We can also breathe in deeply, filling our lungs with healing oxygen, and allow our mind and body to tap into that infinite reservoir of joy that each one of us has within us, no matter our circumstances or our bank accounts.

When we exist in that strong, firmly-rooted, balanced center within us, there's no jealousy over someone else's bank account or achievements. Nothing shakes us.

We are in a state of bliss, too mesmerized by the beauty and variety and richness of our lives to think about anyone else, except to wish them the best.

Let's get rid of the word "work" in our vocabulary. Let's change it to "play." There doesn't have to be "chores," "tasks" or "responsibilities" either. They can be called "kindness games," "loving our family," and, "caring for ourselves and others." That's why we do those things anyway, out of love and compassion for ourselves, our family and friends, our communities, and all the beings we share this planet with.

We can go on a very difficult journey in peace. We can strive hard with joy. We can do stressful things with exuberance. We can love our life, improve our health, and even work ten times longer and more effectively if we can find the joy that exists within every single moment.

Life is too short and unpredictable to delay happiness. No matter what we are going through, happiness is always available. All we have to do is realize that it doesn't lie in some imagined future, some idyllic past, or some far away place.

When we stay present and focused on what's in front of us, all that remains is a feeling of happiness for ourselves, happiness for others, and we can finally break free from any mental resistance to what we have to do. This helps us work smarter, work better, be more creative, and ultimately be more successful.

Achieving Success While Maintaining Our Inner Peace

Someone once asked me, "If life is not fair, why does God want us to play fair?" This is a question that comes up more and more as we see unethical people succeeding in society and getting further and further ahead. It can appear that everywhere we look, the people willing to do anything and hurt anyone have all the good fortune.

These observations make us question if we should be living by the rules. Religions, governments, and society all tell us to live by a set of rules that many people simply do not follow.

So what is the best path forward? Can we be successful and hold onto our values? The root of these questions goes to the heart of the problem: putting more value on material wealth than we do on spiritual wealth.

A saint and a sinner will both die at the end of their lives. They both are heading to the same destination. Who is to say the sinner had a better life than the saint? Who is to say that a person who treats others with cruelty, and who has to stuff down their inner misery with as many pleasures as they can possibly consume in order to not feel pain and guilt, has a better life than a saint with a clean conscience?

Compare a bitter, hateful, hated wealthy tycoon, with a saint who has found inner peace, joy and compassion from helping others.

The saint has no worries about being caught by people they've cheated, and they spend their lives creating meaningful relationships and pursuing their purpose, not money alone.

There is a reason that *The Godfather Part III* is about the mafia family trying to get into a legitimate business. It's because they know that living with a burden on your shoulders is no life at all, and it is never worth your inner peace.

When you live an open and honest life, you have no secrets, you have no shame. That reward alone is greater than any ill-gotten gains.

So it's not that life is unfair. And it's not that God wants us to play fair. It's that we have seen time and time again that it is in our best interest to live an honest life, quite simply because it's the only way to have a peaceful life.

Even though we're all going in the same direction to the same destination, the path we take makes all the difference.

It can be a pleasant and peaceful journey. Or it can be a dark path where we always have to look over our shoulders.

Having the best life has nothing to do with having the most stuff. There's no prize at the end for having had the most riches. But if we're lucky and loving, we'll be surrounded by our loved ones at the end.

The best life is a content life.

That doesn't mean we can't be ambitious. But it does mean working towards big goals with full presence.

Some people do have advantages based on where they were born and what family they were born into. But no matter who you are, we all have to accept where we are. Set conscious and ambitious goals and strive to achieve them with your full attention on the present moment.

No one has to follow man's laws or God's laws. But if we break man's laws, there is the inner turmoil of worrying about being caught. We risk bringing upon ourselves jail time, revenge, or the shame of our community.

If we break God's law — that golden rule — we may find ourselves surrounded by like-minded, greedy, unkind people. And so, we live a life of cruelty surrounded by cruelty, where no one is honest and everyone's suspicious. The love and compassion is gone from our life, relationships become transactional, discussions are negotiations, and kindness is leverage.

Breaking either set of laws has potential upsides, but it also has guaranteed drawbacks. A mind consumed by greed, selfishness, craving and cruelty is not a peaceful, happy mind. When we bring enough consciousness and mindfulness to these difficult questions of morality, a wise answer clearly emerges. That answer, of course, is to choose a life of peace and honesty. It's selfish to be selfless! Because by putting out peace and honesty, we get so much more back in return.

Are We Truly Happy?

It's easy to think we're happy when we have our phones out, eating or drinking our favorite things, listening to a podcast or watching TV. But how long can you sit with yourself? 5 minutes? 20? Can you be happy and content after an hour?

This is how we find the true measure of our inner happiness. This is where we see, underneath the surface, our real nature. This will expose whether we are genuinely at peace, or if we need to work on it.

How we feel under the surface subtly impacts every aspect of our lives. If we lack inner peace, we may unconsciously do everything we can to avoid stillness and silence. We may addictively chase pleasures and external stimuli to our own detriment. We may bottle up our emotions, only to let them eat away at us, or until we explode in rage.

This is why developing a daily practice of meditation can radically transform our lives. Or even setting some time aside each day to sit quietly alone looking out the window. The more we practice being and not doing, the more we're able to do and the happier and more at peace we'll be.

Where Does True Happiness Come From?

For many of us, for most of our lives, we search for happiness in the world. We look for it in success, in material or financial gains, in partners, in travel, and in experiences. At some point, most of us will come to the realization that we are not happier despite our successes.

When we realize happiness lies within, everything changes. We can enjoy pleasures without craving. We can love without attachment. We can even appreciate difficulties without resistance, inner conflict or stress.

When we stop grasping at external temporary conditions for our happiness, only then can peace and happiness arise. When we start realizing the inner strength, wisdom, calm and peace within us, we can finally experience a lasting permanent joy far beyond anything brought on by something outside of us.

Fans of *Star Wars* may recall a quote which was originally borrowed from the *Bhagavad Gita*, where Yoda says, "Fear is the path to the dark side. Fear leads to anger, anger leads to hate, hate leads to suffering."

That line is as true in a galaxy far, far away, as it is in the *Gita* from a time long, long ago.

By dwelling on sense objects — those things we can see, hear, taste, smell and touch — we develop an attachment and desire for them. When those desires are not fulfilled, we get angry. Not only do we get angry, but even if those desires are fulfilled, they will inevitably lead to more cravings, more dependence, lower highs and lower lows.

That's the way addiction works. It doesn't even matter if it's to a drug or activity like gambling, any extreme desire creates the same disturbance within us. Whether it's overindulgence or under-indulgence where we're fighting incredibly hard to resist temptation, pain follows desire. Only a balanced, peaceful approach can find that middle path, where we can enjoy the pleasures of this world without creating the disturbing desire for those objects. We can enjoy them without losing ourselves, we can indulge with awareness, and we can simultaneously engage in something while mentally preparing ourselves for its inevitable end.

If we continue seeking sense objects without having developed a peaceful, harmonious mind, anger follows (like what happens when a child has their iPad taken away). From that anger, delusion arises because these desires consume our whole lives. We become oblivious to how our addiction is hurting others, and we completely miss the truth: that happiness comes from within and that we don't need those external, physical objects for our happiness. From delusion, confusion enters because we misremember our past and justify our improper behavior and actions because only the desire matters. From confusion comes a loss of reason.

Without reason, we are lost and chaos takes over our lives. When we move away from our centered, balanced nature, this is when mental health issues such as depression, anxiety, debilitating fear, and addiction take a firm hold in our lives. Only the self-controlled meditator can develop the passivity of mind to appreciate everything in life free from likes, dislikes, judgments, opinions and labels. They can be fully at peace, enjoying the good times without attachment, and maintaining their peace through the bad times because they know they are impermanent too.

All sorrows come to an end, but the deep peace that resides in all of us is so profound and joyful that no sorrow can diminish it. No pleasure can compare to inner peace and freedom. The more we search for happiness, the further it gets. Only by entering a state of stillness and allowing for reflection and contemplation, can wisdom arise, can clarity be found, and a lasting happiness and peace can be achieved.

Life Lesson 8

Life is an Illusion

During my time at a Buddhist monastery high up in the Himalayan Mountains, I found a book in the library called, <u>Becoming Your Own Therapist</u>, by a prominent Buddhist monk, Lama Yeshe. To me, that book first showed me what spirituality can be. When you realize that life is an illusion, that everything is one, and that everything has meaning because we project meaning onto it, then you can awaken from the rollercoaster of life, step off and appreciate and marvel at the engineering of the roller coaster, noticing the beautiful complexities of life, instead of feeling so attached and consumed by them.

We all know we should enjoy the journey, but that's easier said than done. Sometimes we get so attached to a desired outcome that we are not present during the process and we miss it entirely.

The fact is, we don't perform tasks as well when they are purely a means to an end. We don't fully dig in and commit ourselves to each step in the process.

When we realize that there actually is no destination, that life keeps marching on even after a goal is achieved, only then can we realize that the journey is everything.

So often, we work so hard towards something thinking it will bring us happiness, only to later discover that we got the thing but not the happiness.

We think happiness is a house, spouse, kids, cars and vacations. But how many people have those things and are still unhappy? It's not the goals that matter, it's the process. It's not what we have, it's how we have them. Are we appreciative or do we spend all our time thinking about the success we don't yet have?

Understanding impermanence on a deep level, to truly be aware of it and fully understand it at all times, rids the mind of any ability to experience loss, grief, sorrow, and attachment. When we believe temporary things will last forever, we suffer.

Only the nonmaterial, empty space, and field of consciousness which pervades the universe, is permanent, eternal and infinite. Everything else is like a magic trick, an illusion, here one minute and gone the next.

Only the way in which we experience the journey matters. Take someone who wants to write screenplays for the movies. His whole life, he's been a struggling screenwriter. He's written tons of movies but nothing's gotten made, except for maybe a few small independent films.

Compared that person to someone else who's written 10 or 20 huge blockbuster movies. Both of them spent their lives following their passion, writing dozens of screenplays, and living each day exactly how they wished. Each of them spends their days doing what they love.

The only difference between them is the money in their bank account, how big their house is, and how fancy and expensive the things are that surround them. So what really matters in life? The fancy stuff we don't need and won't appreciate anyway, or actually living the life of our dreams?

Even if you don't achieve your dreams, following your dreams is living the dream.

There are no destinations, only pitstops. So many people think that when they get their next promotion, they'll be able to enjoy their life. Then the promotion comes and they realize everything's the same. They don't know how to be happy because they've put it off for so long. They thought it was something they can't have until a certain point, and then life passed them by. When they look back on their life, they'll see they didn't appreciate the time they had.

At the end of our human journey, when we cast off these bodies, our possessions and achievements will not be coming with us. In the end, we will all lose everything. But there is liberation in that fact, because it reminds us that what actually matters is the presence, love and happiness we shared.

Whatever is temporary is a mere illusion, yet we spend so much time stressing and obsessing about these illusory perceptions. The more we expand our consciousness to this fact, the less significance all this temporary stuff will have.

Humans mistake nearly every situation we find ourselves in as permanent.

We can feel an emotion so strongly that we're certain we'll feel it forever, even though 10 minutes later we'll most likely be feeling something completely different. When we live in our head, everything feels like forever because that's what the voice in our head usually says.

For example, we can eat too much food at a meal and say to ourselves, "I am never eating again. I don't think I'll ever be hungry ever again!" We naturally think every current state is forever. This lies at the root of our innate tendency to constantly grasp onto the past and try to hold it in our hand for as long as possible, only to have it fall through our fingers like sand.

We can repeatedly wake up from a hangover and say, "I never want to drink again," only to want another drink a few hours later, each time realizing how foolish we were to think that the feeling would last.

But we'll keep saying it and keep reliving our conditioned patterns because we are still under this illusion of permanence. We are living in time instead of in the eternal present, and so we are not consciously responding to the world, we are unconsciously reacting.

We have to accept the constant change of our universe on a deep level, not simply on a conscious level, but in our subconscious and unconscious minds as well.

Only then can we peacefully welcome all of the things that come into our life without desire or aversion. And, we can let them go peacefully when they leave, with no attachment or clinging.

To do this, we have to reconnect with and recognize our true nature, which is the unchanging consciousness within us. Stillness is our gateway to the present moment. **Only from stillness can we perceive change.**

So we have to tap into that stillness within, beyond thoughts, and exist in that inner space where life exists beyond form, beyond our names and identities and personalities. We are stillness, which is why we can perceive both change and stillness. We are the space from which these bodies emerged. We are this eternal present moment. We are the universe.

Our thoughts are constantly changing. Our emotions are constantly changing. The cells in our body are constantly dying and new ones are being born. Yet our consciousness is the only thing that has never changed in our entire life. Consciousness is the continuum that despite everything else changing, despite the body being completely replaced with new cells every seven years (more or less), and despite our personalities completely changing over the course of our lifetime, we are still the same people.

Our stream of consciousness is the one constant, unchanging presence in our lives. It is our true selves, the root of who we are, the knowing presence within. Even though our eyesight may fade, our hearing may go, and our memories may disappear, our consciousness is never diminished.

If we are alive — even when we're asleep — we are conscious. We cannot be unconscious because that would mean we lack the awareness of nothing. But that is what dreamless sleep is: the awareness of nothingness.

The more present we are, the more we shift from a person with a name to that witnessing eternal presence. We move beyond all thoughts, all notions of our identity, all notions of who we should be and what we should have and how our lives should be. We move past that constantly commenting mind, and we move into the deeper reality — the permanent, everlasting, eternal, infinite space, which is the most real thing in our universe and makes all of existence possible. It cannot be burned, destroyed, damaged or affected in any way whatsoever.

Everything that is illusion is constantly in change, constantly coming into existence and falling out of existence. When we cling to the mind and its chaotic thoughts, we lose our grip with reality, our own inner stillness, and the stillness that's always around us.

We live in a universe where every object is made out of entirely empty space. Atoms are made of smaller subatomic particles which are infinitely small points of space that only appear to have the qualities of mass, but actually have no weight or size. It's more like vibrating, highly concentrated energy that appears as solid matter to us.

What is real in this illusion is the space from which it emerges and the space to which it returns.

The more we sit in that space of stillness, that space of consciousness, the more stillness and peace we bring into our lives. This is the world beyond duality and illusions. It is eternally safe and comforting.

The more we move past that commenting brain and we practice being and witnessing, the more good things can enter our lives because we have the space to receive them without attachment, we can let go with gratitude, and remain at peace flowing with time.

In this vast inner spaciousness, there is no time. There is no looking back, comparing this moment to the past or some imagined future. There is no bias or conditioning. We are open to reality as it is, welcoming everything that comes and allowing everything to leave. This is the flow state where we are fully present, where our hearts are fully open. This doesn't mean we put ourselves in danger or that we're letting go of our higher wisdom of self-protection.

We usually cling onto our thinking mind because we feel like we need the constant chatter to be smart, to avoid danger, and to get through life. But when we are fully present, we are wiser and safer. We're not going to walk into traffic. We're not going to waste our energy ruminating on the past or future.

In the peaceful space, we're going to be at our optimal state of consciousness because we'll be fully reacting to the present moment and what it is requiring of us without any story in our mind, without being distracted by thoughts or about something happening later. We will realize peace and happiness are always right here, we simply have to stop grasping for it out there in order to find it.

Life Lesson 9

Add More Moments of Wow
in Your Life

We all have spiritual moments throughout our lives. That first moment you see a sunset or a flower, maybe a piece of art, and you say, "Wow." In that moment of true awe and wonder, that childlike wonder that schools usually beat out of us, that is when we're fully present, fully alert, fully appreciative, and there's a real connection between the experience and the experiencer.

Becoming One With the Universe

It's like we've all been wearing super high-definition virtual reality headsets with crystal clear surround sound, and even smell-o-vision, all our lives. It's easy to forget the awe and wonder of this magnificent universe we were born into.

Our brains are physical objects designed to recreate the physical world. But the more we practice being present, the quieter our mind becomes and the more we can listen to our heart and intuition. This is how we tune in to our own inner peace and joy. When we have constant access to that, nothing temporary can aggravate or disturb us.

I have found that in meditation, by closing my eyes and disconnecting from the outer world, I can more deeply connect with our mysterious and miraculous universe. It is like tuning a radio to a specific frequency.

When we're chaotic, we seek out and create chaos. If we're angry, violent movies and video games may speak to us. But if we're peaceful, our lives become peaceful.

When we look up from our phones and gaze at the night sky, we are looking into infinity. It's the only place we can do that. It's similar to closing our eyes in meditation because we see the blackness and we can feel a sense of the infinite vastness within us as well — a bodiless, massless consciousness looking out into nothingness. Pure peace and stillness.

It is a very spiritual experience to look at the stars. That mesmerizing, transformative, quality time of communion with the universe is our natural way of being and birthright. It truly is a meditation to put our phones away and look at the stars.

Most people today in technologically advanced societies have a very strong urge to fill up any space of time with the most stuff possible. We are consumers. Even in meditation, people are filling up the space with music, mantras, binaural beats, crystals, Buddha or Jesus statues, apps, blindfolds, brain scanning devices, or guided meditations where someone talks the whole time.

While all of these meditations can be helpful and may have their place in your meditation routines, this drive to fill up space is emblematic of a culture that has been conditioned to believe that happiness comes from stuff, that enjoying ourselves is a waste of time, and to resist stillness, peace and spaciousness.

Furthermore, I know a lot of people will say that swimming is their meditation, or painting or jogging or dancing. But all of these activities are meditative, not meditation.

They are incredibly important activities for our mental health and wellbeing. They make life worth living and they bring us into the present moment. But, they don't fundamentally change the way we think and experience the world after the activity is over.

In classical sitting meditation, we sit still, close our eyes, and observe either our breath or body. It takes a still body to create a still mind.

By practicing staying present, it becomes a habit. This extended focus on our breath or body improves our focus, increases our patience, expands our awareness to the subtle sensations in our body, which then translates as expanded awareness into every aspect of our life. We see more, we understand more, and a sense of security and peacefulness emerge.

We humans are so funny. Even looking up at the stars

isn't enough for us anymore. Now we want to get out our stargazing app, take a photo, learn the constellations and label everything, instead of being with the sky, seeing it, and truly taking it in. How long can we spend looking up before we get bored? A few minutes? A few seconds? There truly are few things more spiritual that we can do than lay on our back in the grass or on a bench, and watch the stars for an hour or two. It is an incredible experience.

We quite literally expand our consciousness by looking up and putting our size and place in the universe into perspective.

When we look down and around us, we feel like our lives and this moment are the most important things in the world. We get so caught up in our desires that we can't enjoy the blessings in our lives.

But when we look up, we see we're ants on an ant hill, insignificant compared to this overwhelmingly awe inspiring universe.

Our worries become insignificant, a rude waiter is insignificant, traffic and bad weather and spilling coffee on our shirt before the big meeting, all become irrelevant under the weight of oneness.

If you don't have stars where you live, you can watch a sunset. If you can't see the sunrise, lay in the park looking at the clouds. If there is no park, try a plant. And if there are no plants, we always have direct access to the infinite within us. Everyday, all around us, is beauty and wonder. We just have to look up from our phones to notice.

Our purpose of life is to live and live it fully.

We have one short life and it would be a shame to miss it.

To experience each moment fully, not lost in the past or worrying about the future, we have to pay attention.

All there is is the journey. There is no destination because death is not a place, it is the beginning of a new journey. So we better enjoy this universe while we're here.

We are not these temporary bodies. We are the lifeforce energy or consciousness. The difference between a dead body and a living one is the animating energy, and it's the same in every one of us, passed down in an unbroken chain 4 billion years ago. That is the stuff that makes us who we are. That is what we loved about the people we lost.

All the knowledge and wisdom of the universe is in each and every one of us. We don't have to read any book or belong to any religion to discover our true nature, we only have to look within. This world was made for us, and we were made by it.

Enjoying Things That Bring More Presence to Your Life

Nature, in all of its forms, is an access point to the wonder and beauty and majesty of our lives.

Whether it's a tree, a flower, a bird, a pet or a baby, what we're looking at is presence looking back at us through these beings who don't know the insanity of living in the past or future, constantly worrying, confused, insecure, burned out, angry, jealous or greedy. They are pure peace, patience, presence, kindness and joy. This is of course our true nature as well, which we can rediscover.

Art is another one of these beautiful access points that can take us into presence and stillness and help us see the wonder and beauty in the world, creating beauty, and sharing it. We can even observe and appreciate the craftsmanship of a handmade item and get a feel for the person who made it and what they were experiencing, and we can feel a sense of deep connection.

Everything can become an access point to the present moment when we observe it carefully without labels, as if we're seeing it for the first time, admiring and appreciating it, taking in all the details as if we were going to paint it later from memory.

For much of our lives we do things as a means to an end. We brush our teeth in order to have clean teeth, we eat a meal in order to fill our stomachs, and we clean the house in order to have a clean house — all so we can be done with the task. But when we focus on the end goal, we miss out on the activity, and we further develop a permanent mindset that causes us to miss out on our whole lives.

When we become present, when we inhabit our body with consciousness, we find we can actually enjoy all of the things we've been mentally trying to escape from.

When we are always lost in our head instead of present, we're subconsciously training our mind that life is bad, boring, and worthy of escape.

To always be thinking trains our mind to never be satisfied and always be racing, which makes us feel exhausted, overwhelmed and negative.

We think our life determines our thoughts, but our thoughts determine our life.

When we bring consciousness and awareness into every activity we do, when we fully chew and taste our food and feel all the textures of each bite, and when we feel every step we take during a walk, we're training our mind to find the beauty in life in the present moment. Intention becomes infused with every action we take. We are no longer mindlessly reacting to the whims of society. Instead, we are fully enlightened beings: present, conscious, and acting with intention and purpose. As our actions, words and thoughts come into alignment, our lives become filled with joy, love and peace.

Silence is a doorway to peace and opportunity. To be able to sit quietly, observing our chaotic mind, and allowing it to settle down and meet in that stillness, is an incredible gift. Because there is silence, stillness and space, there is life. Without space, there could be no existence. Without silence, there could be no differentiating the sounds we hear. And while we may be incredibly focused on the sights and sounds we experience, by shifting some of our awareness to the space between objects and the silence underneath the sounds, it can bring a newfound level of peace to our lives.

Life Lesson 10

God And the Universe are One

God and the universe are really interchangeable words. The universe loves us/God loves us. Have faith in the universe/have faith in God. It's all the same. If God is everywhere, then God is the universe and there cannot be one particle separate from God. And the beauty is, you don't have to believe in God to believe in the universe.

Everything always works out in the universe. The universe is a miraculous design. The universe is omnipresent and omniscient. It provides not just the delicious foods that nourish us, but the beauty and majesty of the stars, the mountains, flowers and waterfalls. It was kind of an easy thing to realize that universe oneness is what uni means.

We live in a universe of energy, and Einstein showed us that matter is energy. What is that energy? And where did it come from if not itself? If the energy came from any other place, that would only lead to further questions, such as, "If it came from someplace else, where did that place get the energy from?"

God/the universe/energy is in every single atom, neutron, electron, and in the space between them. These mystifying, microscopic particles that contain enough energy to cause a nuclear explosion, that hold all matter together and allow for all life to exist, are infused with the beauty, power, mystery and divinity of our incredible universe. In every corner of this universe, from the very large to the very small, lies the miraculousness of our existence.

So it doesn't matter what name you use. God/the universe doesn't have a name because who would've named it? Humans did that. But, we ended up mistaking the names for the truth.

While the laws of physics may differ from the spiritual laws, they are bound together in an eternal embrace. The laws of gravity and electromagnetism may govern our physical universe, but the spiritual laws of cause and effect (karma) and impermanence are tied directly to the physical laws. The spiritual, nonphysical, conscious energy of our universe gave rise to the physical laws, not the other way around. **Intention precedes action, and quantum mechanics shows us that consciousness precedes matter** (See the Double-Slit Experiment for reference).

The spiritual gives way to the physical, and the physical gives way back to the spiritual. This is our infinite, eternal nature. This loving energy, which we all are, has given us this incredibly beautiful planet we live on. It has given rise to all life on this planet, and sustained each and every one of us.

God is love.
God is gratitude.
God is forgiveness.
God is compassion and kindness.
God is our trust in the universe that everything will work out, that there's a purpose.
God is creativity — the creative spirit inside all of us. That is why we have creation, why there is something instead of nothing, and why we all have a drive inside of us to build a beautiful life.

It does not matter what you call it— the universe, universal consciousness, creativity, God, or even aliens — the name we use is only a sound pointing towards the truth. What matters is living in alignment with the fundamental laws of this universe. Because there is cause and effect, because actions do have consequences, and because we gravitate towards where our energy goes, it's objectively better to practice love, compassion, peace and joy so their impact can spread like a ripple in the water.

Is There a God or Not?

When I was a little kid, growing up in a reformed Judaism household, I was having a hard time believing the stories from the *Bible*. When I was maybe seven or eight years old, I came home from Sunday school and I said to my dad, "Did Moses really part the Red Sea? Did all those miracles really happen?"

He replied, very honestly, "Well, maybe they're metaphors, maybe it didn't happen exactly like that. I know the *Bible* says the Earth was created in seven days, but maybe seven days to God is more like 7 billion years. Maybe the Red Sea was shallow and the Egyptians drowned with their heavy armor, but the Israelites were able to swim across."

Even though he was honest with me, my internal reaction was, "Whoa, my teachers lied to me. They never said this was a metaphor. They said the *Bible* is what literally happened. They didn't say, like my dad said, that maybe the Jews escaped Egypt at low tide. They said Moses lifted his staff, slammed it down, and parted that sea like a wizard."

From that moment on, I realized adults lie and I vowed never to trust them (often this was at my own peril, and often at adults' great frustration, but something about mindfully verifying, analyzing, experimenting and exploring every notion, fact and idea spoke to me).

From that day forward, I was a rebel without a cause. Anything that anyone told me, I had to figure out for myself if it was true.

That was the day I even became an atheist. Right after my bar mitzvah, I told my parents, "I'm not Jewish anymore and I am an atheist." I was a handful.

At the time, I was 100% sure that this old book was full of made-up stories. When I got a little older, at about 25, I was still pretty sure that there was no God, that atheism was right, and that the idea of God wasn't as convincing as my science books.

I felt pretty certain there wasn't some guy in the sky with a white beard saying the things that were in the *Bible*, like that we should treat our slaves well and murder our disobedient children. But, by this slightly more mature time in my life, I realized the real truth: nobody knows.

I may have leaned towards atheism, but even I had to

admit uncertainty. We have to be honest with ourselves. The truth is, nobody knows.

Nobody has died, taken a video camera with them, videotaped God, and then came back to life and showed us all the tape. So nobody has any evidence for it, and nobody has any evidence against it. The story may sound fishy, but nobody knows.

But ultimately it comes down to this: why believe anything? Because mystery is too scary? Mystery is the truth, and Jesus said, "The truth will set you free." We can only believe in things we know nothing about, otherwise it would be called knowing.

It's OK to not know, but if we don't know what we don't know because we wanted to believe a beautiful story, then we're only going to get further from the truth, subconsciously train our mind to believe that the unknown universe is scary and dangerous, and we will use our religion to alleviate the stress caused by the religious dogma that makes us afraid.

Later on in my thirties, when I was living in Hindu ashrams in India, I was struck by their belief in millions of gods. Later when I went to live with shamans in South America, some of whom admired Jesus and the Hindu Gods as well, I came to the conclusion that you can both believe in God because you see the numerous benefits that come with it and so you choose your beliefs, and you can still acknowledge that nobody knows.

We can keep these two concepts in our head at the same time. We can say to ourselves, "Rationally, I choose to believe that God will heal me because that will activate my placebo effect and cause me to literally heal faster.

I choose to believe in the all loving universe that is always looking out for me, even when it's hard to realize, so that I will have more peace, more love, more gratitude, and more faith that everything will work out."

You can even say "universe" if "God" is too foreign a concept. You can interchange God and the universe in pretty much every sentence. It doesn't matter what you call it, but there is no denying it. Scientists say everything came from nothing, but that nothing was everything.

To Believe or Not to Believe

It actually doesn't matter if there's a God or not. Nobody knows if there is, and what would change if there was or wasn't? Nothing.

But, I'm going to choose to believe in God, while still simultaneously acknowledging that I have no clue. I'm going to choose to believe because it's one more thing to be grateful for.

It's one more thing to feel love towards. It's one more thing to make me feel like everything will work out just fine and that we're always looked after. To know that if we ask for healing, we'll receive healing. If we need anything, our needs will be met. One more reason to release any little stress that we carry. To have faith in this loving universe creates a happier, more loving, more hopeful sense of being.

This isn't delusion either. This is based on a deep understanding into the nature of our universe. From quantum mechanics to the interconnected nature of reality, it is clear that this universe is one, it is beyond our understanding, and it is conscious.

Like a computer turns on when electricity flows through

it, our bodies turn on with consciousness because it flows around us and through us.

The debate about whether there is a God or not misses the point. The real question is: are you more likely to heal — and heal quicker — from a disease if you believe that God, the universe, or prayer are real?

And the answer is a resounding yes. The placebo effect is so powerful, one study found that women who were prayed for had twice as many pregnancies as women who were not prayed for. In multiple studies, a sugar pill cured people's cancer because they were told it was a miracle cure.

The placebo effect is a very real and often misunderstood phenomenon. It's not a mystery. It is proof that the human body can heal from anything if it believes it will.

This further shows that most or all illness is created by our fears, worries and doubts — negative beliefs (not necessarily directly, but it could be that the stress weakened our immune system). Positive beliefs and faith, on the other hand, heal us.

If anyone tells you they know there's a God for certain, or if they know exactly with certainty what happens when you die, run! The truth is, nobody knows.

There is nothing wrong with believing in these things, as long as we can address the eternal, ultimate truth — that nobody knows.

If we can all humble ourselves and admit that we don't know all the answers, but that we choose to believe because it connects us to a deeper level of love and gratitude, then these divisions of hatred between the various religions can cease to exist because we all will understand, "Yes, I believe this. But I also think what you believe could be true and I don't have all the answers."

It's beautiful to believe. It's a powerful, impactful, and uplifting part of human nature that has brought peace and solace to billions. But, a delusion, especially a self-delusion, is not going to be all positive. Delusion is not the goal, not a virtue, and not a path to true, lasting, universal peace.

Delusion is dependent on blind faith, but when you can be honest with yourself, when you can look at your beliefs and examine them closely and truthfully, you can have an unshakable faith based on confidence, and an unshakable hope for the future. When we don't explore our beliefs with honesty, we're more likely to have a crisis of faith and become lost.

Jesus said in the *Bible* "The truth will set you free." But I think the next line he said after that accidentally got lost in all the Bible pages, but If we had the full transcript, I believe he said, "...and the truth is, nobody knows." Much like Gandhi said in his book, *My Experiments With Truth*, "**Truth is one, paths are many**"

As Gandhi conducted his experiments to discover what was the ultimate truth, he was also finding his own truth and how to be true to himself. It's important to remember that **everyone's truth is true to them, and even though they may be on a different path or a different place on the same path, their truth is theirs.**

Too often, we get hung up on God's name, people's religious affiliations, and stories that were meant to be metaphors. But like Gandhi, we can find our own truth, and if it creates harmony, mutual cooperation and peace, we'll know we're on the right track.

As long as we recognize the fundamental truth that this is only *my* truth, then we can respect and honor the beliefs of others. We can live in a global, unified, and higher level of conscious awareness that celebrates our differences instead of dividing us.

Can Religion and God Help Us Reach Our Ultimate Potential?

What role do rituals, traditions, and religious communities have in an individual's path to spiritual awakening? Can religion help us reach our ultimate potential? Or, are they nothing but superstitions and fairy tales? Do they create positive outlets for spiritual growth, or do they simply further divide our already-divided planet?

We see all the time in the news, stories of priest wrongdoing. We see stories of ideological extremists in certain parts of the world causing destruction. And we even see a rise of cults and extremist groups popping up all over our own countries. We can begin to wonder, is this religion thing doing more harm than good? Is it dividing us more than it is creating connection? Is it building the foundations of universal love, or irrational thinking?

Some people may wonder, do the religions and superstitions that we grew up with as children cause us to forgo rational thinking later on in life. Do they suggest that we can let go of critical thinking and reasoning, and that it's OK to believe in magic or superstition or mythology? Is that the kind of supernatural upbringing that enables people to fall for cults and extreme ideologies when they're older?

To answer these questions, first we need to examine and explore our beliefs and why we believe them.

Second, we need to ask ourselves what we're hoping to gain or benefit, and if we are able to get it from other sources.

Third, we can ask ourselves what an ideal religion would look like if we were starting from scratch. What kind of belief system would we want to set up that does the most good and the least harm? Then, we can see if a particular faith or religion falls in line with that kind of value system, or if our faith is opposing it.

While the details can vary widely, the core of what most religions teach are essentially the same. What I mean by that is, without religion and spirituality, we think we're nothing more than these physical bodies.

We assume that the thoughts in our head are who we really are. These thoughts pop into our head out of nowhere, and we unconsciously, unintentionally, and often to our own detriment, become lost in negative thoughts for most of our lives.

There are two ways we can deal with constant negative thinking. For one, we can clear our mind of all thoughts, and we can use very extreme practices to do that, such as spending years in meditation, fasting, giving up all material possessions, and living an ascetic lifestyle. Many have completely left society in order to create a situational life where there is no need for thought, and where nothing can distract us from the practice of freeing ourselves from thought.

There have been countless wandering monks and sadhus throughout the East who have given up everything except a bowl and a robe. The bowl is what they ask for food with, and the robe their only clothes. They'll offer spiritual teachings in exchange for food, and they will ask for a meal when they are hungry, and nothing more.

The second way — the middle path — is to **use spirituality or religion to live in the world, but not be consumed by it**. This is what any true belief system will help us achieve. Truth will help us fulfill our earthly duties, responsibilities and roles, but also maintain a peacefulness, joy and playfulness, and ultimately to remember that those roles are not who we truly are.

Just because we live on Earth doesn't mean we shouldn't look up to the stars. Similarly, because we live in this physical universe doesn't mean we need not turn our attention to the infinite. The temporary stuff around us is not the be all and end all of the universe.

The stuff in our little lives doesn't contain the magnitude and magnificence that is life itself. All the stuff we see is simply the way we interact and navigate this world, but it isn't what is most important.

What is most important, is remembering our connection with everything — with God/the universe, with our fellow living beings who we share this planet with — and to never lose that awe and wonder, majesty and mystery that every child and creature has naturally.

When we feel connected, gratitude and love emerge. We cherish the source that brought us into this world, the source that sustains and nourishes us.

We'll naturally want to nourish the world around us and pass on the many blessings we feel. They say, "Happy wife, happy life," which is true. But, a happy world, a VERY happy life. Helping others is what it's all about.

For many people, religion provides that framework to

exist in society. The teachings, the stories, the metaphors, the prayers, all become like new software for the brain that allows space for intentional, conscious, positive thoughts. Instead of unconsciously letting the world fill up our heads, we intentionally fill them with positive messages. And practicing any kind of conscious, intentional thinking is essential for dealing with these brains that, if left undealt with, will be constantly racing, jumping from thought to thought and topic to topic, and always going crazy by imagining the worst possible scenarios for every situation we find ourselves in.

So by creating this mental script outline — this blueprint, this architectural framework for universal love — we can inject positive and hopeful beliefs and attitudes that underlie our daily thinking by framing our existence in a deeply beneficial, beautiful, and meaningful way. It doesn't have to come from religion either. People have found helpful messages in stoicism, ancient mythologies, various philosophies, and even children's books conveying lessons of morality and virtue.

We currently live in a world where the dominant messaging comes from advertisements, TV, movies, music, books, magazines, social media, the news, podcasts and radio — all profit-driven platforms. Churches, temples and mosques have largely become the last institutions for delivering messages aimed at nourishing the soul without the overt goal of profiting off of us.

How incredible would it be if half the billboards reminded us to be more grateful, to take a deep breath, to relax and let go of our stress, to help others and be kinder? Unfortunately, we have zero ads that say that.

But we need those reminders. We need community. It's so wonderful that there are these religious organizations out there, offering people some spiritual help and guidance. But it doesn't have to come from religion. We can start our own communities as well. We can build them around compassion, where every faith is welcome, because division only leads us further from oneness.

At the end of the day, all religions create a point of attention for our awareness to rest on, like how meditation helps us focus on our breath or a mantra or on the present moment.

With their religious stories, their regular holidays and festivals, our mind is given something positive and helpful to keep in our mind, which helps keep our mind from wandering into dark territories.

Because of that, many people find going to church, a mosque, or a temple to be incredibly peaceful, and incredibly transformative, changing how we view the world and how we interact with society.

Of course, the details will be different — the stories, the names of the characters, and the names we use for God or many gods. But at the root, these stories shape how we think and view our lives. It's a structure for understanding the world that creates a sense of stability in our lives.

In a world with too few positive messages, religion can be essential to find some respite and solace. Not to mention, when we walk into a beautiful church or temple or mosque, the inspiration we feel is so profound and measurable that it can have a measurable impact on our brains and our lives. Simply being in a beautiful place, where we're not rushed, where we can take a deep breath, and where we can be inspired and uplifted, is like oxygen to us.

Every religion has its spiritual practices and ceremonies,

whether it's prayer, lighting candles, lighting incense, bowing or chanting, all of these beautiful traditions create opportunities to invite presence into our lives. We don't even have to belong to any religion to take part in all of these rituals if we want to. The benefits are universal. We can be nonbelievers and still enjoy participating in the beauty of these cultures.

Just one moment of presence, one moment between thoughts, is a deeply profound peace. When we're engaging in a ceremony, it brings order and routine to an otherwise chaotic and random life. Rituals and routines are vehicles for setting aside the thinking mind, and instead, peacefully flow through action.

To set aside a couple minutes a day to add some sacred presence into your life is very healing, reassuring, and gives many people a very deep sense of calm, which is so important for our spiritual health and wealth.

And when we combine meditation (the emptying of the mind), with positive messages (the filling of the mind), this is when we see a profound shift take place.

A great deal of research has been done showing the benefits of having daily rituals, and the impact that our beliefs about life have on our psyche. Positive spiritual messages give us hope for the future, and daily rituals give us a sense of predictability and calm during dangerous or uncertain times.

For many people, the idea of belonging to a religion, regularly going to a place of worship, and adopting traditions that they will pass down to future generations, has immense benefits. For others, this path may not speak to them.

In Hinduism, there are four paths of yoga. These are

paths to what they call either enlightenment, liberation, moksha, or finding our true self. It can even be called nirvana, Buddha nature, Christ consciousness, or simply salvation.

These paths all lead us towards reaching our highest level of bliss, and freedom from suffering. We can follow one path, all the paths, any combination of paths, and we can even take them one at a time. There is no wrong way to peace and compassion.

Of the four paths, bhakti yoga is the path of devotion. This path is about expressing love towards a guru, a deity, or many deities. It could even be devotion to the universe, or simply the miracle of existence.

This is the role that religions, temples, churches, mosques and ashrams all fill. By nourishing the sense of loving selflessness, devotees are able to reach and sustain an elevated state.

Through devotion and rituals, the aim is to use a mental image of the object of worship in order to keep pure love in the center of our mind and heart at all times. It's about surrendering our fears and worries over to God, and rediscovering the sacred in everything.

Another path of yoga is called karma yoga, or the path of service and charity to others. Called seva in Hindi, this kind of selfless service makes us dissolve our ego, dissolve our pride, and realize the deepest love there is, which is to recognize others as ourselves.

Jnana Yoga is the path of knowledge and intellect. This path is designed to rid ourselves of ignorance and destructive thinking. A jnana yogi learns scriptures, transcribes them, and turns inward to analyze deeply the nature of our reality and our suffering.

Lastly, raja yoga is the path of meditation. In deep reflection with a calm mind, we can train our mind, master our thoughts and feelings, master our life, and make stillness and presence our way of life.

So fortunately, if religion doesn't call to a person, if no benefit is gleaned, there is a path out there for everyone. Human flourishing is universally available to us. It doesn't have to be from one particular religion or tradition. It can be from many faiths, no faith, or you can create a new one however you want. You have as good a God antenna as any other human. All it requires is turning inward and seeing what is there beyond form.

When I was a young boy and forced to go to temple, I was bored out of my mind. I didn't understand the point. I asked my dad if going to temple makes people happy (they didn't look happy). He said that it's more about connecting with our community and with God, but I didn't feel that. I was forced against my will to put on a suit every Saturday and sit quietly while listening to people speak Hebrew for an hour. I probably needed the lesson in patience, but my ADHD was not having it.

Not everyone is religious for the same reason. Some people may be searching for a community, something that meditation is going to be difficult to fulfill.

And, going to a place of worship is one of the few remaining ways our modern, technologically advanced, socially disconnected society can find a close and supportive community. We do need that. Community is healing.

In places where people live the longest, they have the tightest, closest communities, and every member of the community is valued and feels needed well into old age.

For so many people who live either alone or with their immediate family, often coworkers are the only people we know. Adult friendships have plummeted in recent years.

Opportunities to create a larger community can be very beneficial to mental health, physical health and spiritual health. If you want to sing in a choir or dance or join in festivities, religions and communal spiritual traditions can be essential to fulfilling those needs.

If beautiful culture and rituals fill your soul and lift your spirit, then living in a way that honors those needs could be part of your path.

For some people, seeing cultures celebrate holidays, festivals, perform ceremonial dance and other cultural traditions, is the most beautiful thing they've ever seen.

For others, like how the Dalai Lama once remarked, the pageantry is very boring, and he often falls asleep or talks with people nearby quite disruptively, but he does it with that sweet smile so no one stays too mad at him. It goes to show that we are all different, we all have different needs, and we all are drawn to different paths, but they all do lead to the same truth.

Which brings me back to an important question I posed earlier, "What should religion and spirituality look like if we were starting from scratch? If we knew then what we know now, how would we design the most beneficial, least harmful religion or spirituality?

I think we could all agree that **love should be at the core**, unifying all of us, not humans alone, but all of God's creatures, all of the universe's precious living beings. It would ideally not divide us into groups or spark conflict.

An ideal faith would have the least opportunity for extremists to hijack, by claiming metaphors as literal truth, or myths as factual. We would want it to incorporate all of the paths to liberation and freedom. We would want charity, loving devotion, meditation, wisdom, knowledge and intellectual analysis.

Fortunately, many of our modern religions do provide the space for personal interpretation. They provide space for accepting what speaks to you, and leaving aside what doesn't. They allow for context and an understanding of what society was like when these ancient texts were written and what kind of audience they were speaking to. We can understand and appreciate how at the time these books were written, they were monumental leaps forward in ethics, cleanliness, and knowledge.

The religion we would design today would probably not have worked 2000 years ago when people were sacrificing animals, dying from poor sanitation, killing each other over minor disputes, and generally living in a much different way. In a time when we were still doing human sacrifice, switching to sacrificing animals was surely a positive change, but not one that we'd exactly look back on with pride. Old habits die hard.

But fortunately, the majority of religious people are moderates. They do bring rational thinking to their faith. They are able to understand the context of the time their book was written. Their religious leaders may share many of these more modern reflections of our ideals. So it's not a stretch to imagine that one day we can have a religion that is the source of a tight-knit community, but one where even outsiders feel welcomed, where we can understand that God and soul are interchangeable names for the incomprehensible, unimaginable concepts that we can never fully understand or wrap our heads around on an intellectual level. These words, all the names we use, are of very little importance because **God is not the word God**. God is not words at all. So we can't think about it, we can only feel it. Thoughts and words are nothing more than pointers toward the feeling.

God cannot be understood by the mind but by the heart, these souls, our conscious awareness. Words, thoughts and ideas can even separate us from the truth, because they create an abstraction. Instead of direct experience, we experience the mental interpretation.

If we can remember that these rituals, these names of God, are merely pointers, then there is no reason to attack someone who uses a different pointer to the same truth.

If we can fully understand as a people that the names we use may be different but we are all the children of this universe, the children of God, then we're still brothers and sisters no matter what group we belong to.

When we can see that we are all looking for meaning and that no one has a closer connection to God than anyone else, then we are free to explore and seek truth however we see fit.

The danger is when someone says they speak for God or know God's will. Then a religion turns from looking to God, to looking up to a person. That is where most of the problems arise.

The infinite can not be owned, patented, trademarked or copyrighted. It's free and available to all of us when we quiet our mind enough to hear.

Nearly every faith believes in an omnipresent God, which

means God is the universe, in everything, in every cell and in every breath we take.

If God is everywhere, God is everything.

That means that God and the universe are one, and that we are all God. It means we don't have to go to a temple or a church or a cathedral or a mosque. We can go into a forest. We can go inward, close our eyes, and turn our attention to that source of life and the universe within us, because it's there. It is everywhere. The place we physically go to experience it is not as important as the inner space. Wherever we go, we carry it with us. Spirituality helps us feel it. And that feeling is the source of freedom, salvation, and bliss that all religions and gurus, mystics and saints, shamans and priests are helping us to discover within ourselves.

Life Lesson 11

I Am God. But So Are You.

Every single living being is God / the infinite / the universe. There is no separation between me, you, or God. So treat everyone like God including yourself. And remember, even though you're God, you're no better than anyone else.

I can hear you now, "But Todd, how are serial killers God?"

It is very difficult to see God when people are behaving cruelly, but that is not God consciousness being expressed. That is a conditioned human brain, with infinite potential, but it is disconnected from their heart, disconnected from other people, and shaped by a society that has fed it fear, hatred and violence. Beyond the action, beyond the pain, beyond the trauma and destructive thoughts is universal consciousness, lifeforce energy, and loving presence.

Consciousness is pure love, but the ego is malleable. This adaptability is actually essential for human survival. If we grow up in a cruel world, we may feel the need to develop a hard shell. But if we grow up in a loving world, our consciousness will feel safe to shine through us.

Humans have two modes of operation: being and doing. A flower blooms through being. When our mind is calm, we can do all sorts of things — this is doing through being.

Most of our prisoners didn't grow up in a calm home, they weren't taught how to calm their mind and feel that subtle presence of love and peace within.

And so, they think relief from their inner chaos can only come from satisfying external desires, whatever they may be based on the impulses that pop into our mind.

But when we learn to quiet the mind, sit in stillness, and develop patience, then our higher mind can intervene and we are no longer a slave to the ego.

When we are overcome by desire or anger, we resist reality and we desperately want to change it and we'll be willing to do anything. It's the desperation that makes us waste energy, become angry, make mistakes, and hate the journey. When we are calm, we can do everything with ease and we no longer need to act out.

Perhaps the biggest reason we have cruelty and crime is because people don't know who they truly are. They think they are the violent voice in their head, and so acting on their impulses makes sense to them. Many prisoners even report hearing multiple voices telling them to do things, making it even harder to hear their inner wisdom and intuition. And prisons are so loud too, making it even harder to feel the loving presence of the universe.

To be clear, I am not saying they shouldn't be in prison. People who are a danger to themselves or society must be prevented from doing harm.

But, it's also true that prison doesn't need to be hell either. It can be rehabilitating, and healthy. I often wonder what our society would look like if people who were going through the hardest times were able to get the help they need, almost more like a free university for the least fortunate among us. What if instead of learning how to be better criminals, they were taught meditation, mindfulness, job skills, how to heal and be responsible members of society?

Humans are both pure loving consciousness, and we are the products of our environment because of our adaptive, neuroplastic brains.

Like the world around us, we contain the potential for good and bad. What we nourish, what we focus on, that is up to us. But remember that no one is born in a vacuum or on a deserted island.

Society at large has some responsibility to take for the individuals within it. We see bombs dropped on TV and so it's no wonder guns are on the streets.

When we see the God in everyone, we see the good. And it's important to focus on people's potential when they're showing you the pain from their difficult past.

I know it's hard not to be angry at violence and cruelty,

but anger only perpetuates the cycle. We have to reach deep down, touch that center of love, tap into our powers of forgiveness (not naively or stupidly or dangerously, but with wisdom and safety), see the oneness in all of us, and try our best to break that cycle of pain for future generations.

Sometimes, that love inside of us is difficult to find because we too are disconnected, although not as severely. We may not have been shown the kind of love we deserved. Or maybe the love we were shown was dysfunctional or unhealthy. Maybe we felt too sensitive for this world, and so we disconnected from ourselves for a feeling of safety.

When that loving center is hard to find, and when expressing self-love isn't easy, it's important to remember that we may have built up a hard exterior for safety, but that is not the only way to protect ourselves. We may not have been strong enough as children to face our pain, but we are now.

Today, we have the tools and wisdom to let down our guard, to trust ourselves and the universe, and to stay safe and secure while opening our hearts to the world.

We are all the same eternal, constant, pure consciousness. That constantly racing mind, just because it never shuts up is not who we are. We can quiet it, we can find peace, and we can discover our true selves beyond thought.

The more we do this, the more we will see ourselves in others. So treat everyone with love because they are you underneath the body and temporary thought forms.

We are all exactly the same, only with different shapes and experiences. Both are no fault of any individual.

Even though our genetics and upbringing are beyond our

control, where we put our attention and energy is in our control. If we stop looking outside of us for happiness and choose to discover the infinite source of bliss and love within us, we will surely find it. The day we realize this presence within us, our whole lives become filled with love and joy because we are the radiant source. **Even if we can't always change our circumstances, we can always change the way we perceive them.**

Guests are Gods

When I was living in ashrams and monasteries in India, I was always struck by their hospitality and generosity. When I was leaving one of the Buddhist monasteries, three monks and a nun, whom I became dear friends with, asked me where I was headed to next. I told them I was on my way to Rishikesh a few hours away. One of them said, "Okay, great, we'll take you."

In my mind I was like, "What are you talking about? It's three hours away. That's crazy!"

I assured them that I had been traveling all over India for over a year and would have no trouble getting the bus. They insisted. I said, "Trust me, I'm fine. I can get there myself. But thank you so much, truly."

One of them said, "No, no, we're going there anyway. It's no problem."

I said, "Really?"

And they said, "Yeah, we're going there anyway. We'll all go together, and we'll take you there."

I mean, how could I say no? Going by car did sound better than by bus. So I conceded, "Well alright. If you're all going anyway, let's go!"

So, me and the four monks start walking to the parking lot, but then they keep going and I realize we're headed to the bus stop. No big deal, the bus is great. Plus why would monks have cars?

When we finally got to the city, we all got out and started walking. I asked them what their plans were in the city and how long they were staying. They told me, "Oh, we're going right back."

My mind screamed, "What?!" But my mouth said, "I thought you guys were coming here to visit. You aren't staying?"

They said, "No, we just came to drop you off. Now we're going back."

I told them to at least let me take them to lunch. They accepted. So, we stepped inside a cute little lunch spot right next to us. I was relieved. These guys are so nice, so generous, so thoughtful, and I was so glad I could finally return the favor in some small way by getting them a meal.

We sat down to order and I went to use the restroom because it had been a long bus ride. When I came back, the meal was paid for!?!?! I was almost angry at the incredible generosity and kindness. Flabbergasted, I said, "Are you guys rich or something?"

I didn't think Buddhist monks were rich, which is why I pleaded with them to let me pay them back. Of course they said, "No, no, no. It's our great pleasure to be with you."

This kind of experience wasn't even that uncommon in India. So many people were extremely friendly and even invited me into their homes for food and tea. Being unfamiliar with that level of kindness, I suspiciously thought half of them wanted to kill me and the other half wanted to rob me.

But this generosity, hospitality, and treating everyone like God is an actual way of life in India.

This experience became a lesson for me. What I thought was me being generous and hospitable was more about if it was convenient for me. Even though they wouldn't let me pay them back, I decided I would pass along this kindness to somebody else.

When you're in India, you can't help but notice how little some people have but how much they will give you — food, time, energy. I used to think I was a good host in America, but we have a very independent and isolated culture.

When I stayed at my friends' homes in India, I was never left alone for a minute. They always wanted to see if they could get me anything or take me anywhere. If I wanted to go for a walk, the whole family's coming! It is truly beautiful to experience that kind of community.

I noticed a few times in India, if there was any kind of traffic accident, 100 people would always rush over to make sure everything's okay or to help in any way they can.

Even though it's a billion and a half people, it's a close community. I don't know why that is exactly, but it may have to do with the fact that they say in India, there are more temples than toilets.

In India, unlike any other place I have been, religious and spiritual symbols are everywhere. Every car has a statue of a god on the dashboard. Meditation beads are everywhere. Every house has gods and Sanskrit words adorning the front of the house, and most have many temples inside the home as well.

In India, religion isn't reserved for the temple. It's everywhere because God is everywhere. These daily reminders help us remember that there is something more important than our little lives, our little wants and desires and frustrations. It's a reminder that we are not these finite beings, but we are a part of the infinite. And it reminds us that any guest could be God, so we better treat them accordingly.

Wear the Glasses of Kindness

Love isn't merely a feeling. It's a force of nature that guides us, our species, and our planet. It is more powerful than hate and it alone is the reason we are all here. When we were helpless babies, someone nurtured, cared and provided for each and every one of us.

The more we tune into love, the more we are able to reach our true potential. We are stronger together than we are alone, and love is the glue that builds community and strengthens ourselves and others.

But when we love some but not others, that's not true love, it's partial, dualistic, divided love. That's why universal love — that love for everything and nothing — is the truest form of love there is.

A lot of people think unconditional love is the highest type of love. But actually, if we look at it closely, unconditional love is still conditional.

Most people say, "I love my child unconditionally," but they only love that child on the condition that they're their child. So the question is, can you love a stranger? Can you love a prisoner? Can you love when it's hard? And can you realize that there's only oneness and love in this universe? Everything else is just pain expressed — pain because we lost our connection to that love inside us.

Everything good in our lives came from the laws of physics that govern our universe. Those governing laws that turned energy into stars and planets and people, aren't a trick or a cruel joke. It's love. That's why even in sadness, even in cruelty and pain, there is love. It's not to torture us, it's to teach us. **Life is not a test, it's a lesson.**

When we act from a place of universal love, our true self comes out — wise, patient and kind. Once we recognize the oneness in all things, all that remains is love.

To hate others is to hate ourself. Whether we hate others or hate ourself, there's still hate in our heart. It's the same emotion, so why carry that burden? Why not open up our hearts to love instead?

Universal love is not a feeling or an emotion. It's the innate drive to care for, nurture and protect all those we love, as well as the planet and the animals. But that's not enough. We also have to love future generations and protect their world. And we have to honor the generations who came before us by being good stewards of the Earth for the next generation.

Every decision we make should be made out of love, compassion, and kindness. But **kindness is not the same as niceness.**

Niceness is when we see someone doing something wrong, but we don't want to hurt their feelings so we don't tell them to stop. That's not being kind to that person though.

Kindness is helping that person learn. Niceness is fearfully trying to avoid confrontation or hurting their feelings. Kindness comes with responsibility. Kindness has love at its true core. Niceness has fear. Kindness is courageous. Niceness is about my feelings and creating a situation where I can feel the best. Kindness is about the other person, and also being kind to ourself. It means sometimes engaging in very difficult conversations in order to create a more lasting and positive change. Niceness is about how I can have an easy moment now, but have a harder life in the long run.

When we are kind, we're no longer going to shut up, try to be unnoticed, and walk around on eggshells. Niceness may let people walk all over us, but no one can take advantage of us if we are being kind to ourself.

If someone is trying to take advantage of us, by calling that person out, we may help that person change their life, and we may even prevent someone else from being a victim of that person's cruelty. Whereas being nice would encourage them to continue disruptive, disharmonious behavior. So the truly kind thing to do is to help everybody be their best selves, including ourself.

When we can look at everything through a kindness lens, we'll see that where we've failed is in our cruelty. **We'll never regret being too kind.** We all have moments in our lives where we act in a way we regret. It's usually when we've lashed out at someone, lost our temper, or got caught doing something that is beneath how we portray ourself to be.

But we'll never look back and say, "I was too kind." If we all decided to make kindness the goal — that wise, courageous, patient type of kindness — the world would look like a very different place.

Life Lesson 12

The Universe Created Itself to Experience Itself

We will all live on because life and the universe live on. It's all the same energy and it will go on forever. Space and time are infinite and eternal, and so we too must be, existing in an endless cycle, like all things in this universe, going from matter to energy and energy to matter, from the finite to the infinite and back again.

Life is a miracle. Only one planet in our cosmic neighborhood has it. The fact that atoms arranged themselves into us is insane. We are miraculous, mysterious, more advanced than our best computers. Yet, we walk around stressed, scared, and insecure.

All you have to do to tap into that infinite source of beauty and amazement is to close your eyes, turn your attention inward, and breathe to experience the deep peace and overwhelming bliss and love when you become pure awareness. Simply observe whatever arises with your full attention and you can tap into the essence of pure consciousness.

The more we shift our consciousness to that wise and peaceful observer within, the more those moments of bliss can come into our lives, and the longer those moments become. Pretty soon, our doing becomes infused with being. We flow with time like a river, holding onto nothing, and letting go of everything in every moment. Our actions become more effective because we resist, avoid, and fear nothing.

When we identify with these bodies instead of the energy, we shrink into fear, greed and hate. When we recognize that it's not the bodies we love about our friends and family, but rather their energy, then the truth can start to be seen and a fearless safety and contentment can emerge.

If not on this planet, then on other planets and in other universes, life will go on experiencing the universe as the universe intended forever — and we are the one life. Existence has no beginning and no end, and like everything else we observe, it moves in cycles. It's actually kind of strange that scientists admit that something cannot come from nothing, except the entire universe. The truth is, before the Big Bang, there was something, and many scientists are now starting to realize this as well.

Even without our human brains and hard work, everything in the universe continues on in perfect balance, happening exactly as it's supposed to.

Even a mighty oak tree grows effortlessly. It's our human ego that makes things out to be difficult. Otherwise, things just are the way they are.

Now, I know that it's hard to see that things are neutral all the time when there's so much suffering in the world, so much poverty and hunger, war and violence.

But these problems are here to show us where we've gone wrong and where we can improve. They show us we need to wake up further and do more towards building a future where everybody can live a fulfilling, safe and beautiful life.

It's hard to see how the violent collision between two planets, or the violent collision between two people's egos, are not bad, and that they're actually part of the perfect tapestry of life. But think about it. We need planets to exist, and so sometimes they will collide. In fact, Earth was formed by two colliding planets. Similarly, we need these egos in order to survive, but sometimes they get over inflated and bump into others. And so if we can see truthfully, we'll see that the "bad stuff" led to the best stuff.

How can life evolve into complex human beings without death? How can life arise in the universe if the universe is not alive? And how can consciousness arise in the universe if the universe is not conscious?

Without consciousness, the universe would not exist — this is known as the observer effect which led to the Schrödinger's Cat thought experiment, stating that a cat would be both alive and dead if we were unaware of its condition.

Consciousness is a prerequisite for existence. The universe would only exist as a wave of probability — a quantum field. Only when consciousness perceives this field, does the field collapse into perceived physical matter. A wave of energy, when measured to see where it is, collapses into a physical state, as if it knew it were being watched.

That's why I say the universe created itself to experience itself through us. Many scientists will disagree, some will agree, but it is very clear to me that this is evidence that our **universe is not only conscious, but it is conscious of us.**

14 billion years ago, at the very beginning of our current expansion cycle, we were a tiny ball of plasma — pure energy, like what a lightning bolt is made of — exploding from an infinitely small point space. That plasma cooled down to hydrogen, forming stars, which formed all of the elements that make up our universe.

Today, we are the universe itself, because separation is an illusion. Part of a whole cannot exist without the whole, and no whole can exist without all of the parts.

The wheels are not a car but the car cannot exist without wheels. Likewise, we came from the universe, we are part of the universe, and we are inseparable from it. None of us came from nowhere, born in a vacuum, or created out of thin air.

There is no boundary between you and the universe.

To remember the interconnected nature of everything in the universe, one needs only to look closer at their lunch. Meditate on the sun's rays that evaporated the oceans' water so it could rain down on our crops and grow the plants that made our food or fed the animals that made our food.

Reflect on the farmers who planted and harvested those crops, and the truck drivers who delivered those goods, and all the taxpayers in the country who paid for those roads, and all the road pavers and their family that raised them. Think of the food company workers, the chef, the people who made the plates and utensils, the table makers and the seat makers, the factory workers and the factory engineers. Don't forget the microbial organisms who turned dirt into soil, all our precious insect pollinators, and all the critters and creatures and fungi and rocks that work together to create this habitable planet, this life-sustaining climate, and the perfect air for us.

The entire universe is in your lunch. Every bug and animal, every person — past, present and future — every star, planet and blackhole. Very quickly we will see that there's no separateness, only oneness. Only interconnectedness.

We usually think about bad things happening as isolated events, and we get confused, upset, frustrated and disappointed about them. But when we see the infinite causes that led up to that moment, then a peaceful understanding and acceptance can take place.

We usually see people and things as separate, independently existing phenomena, finite, with a beginning and an end. But when we see their interdependent, interconnected nature, we can no longer blame a person, we can no longer blame ourselves, and we can finally see the infinite and the eternal everywhere we look.

Life Lesson 13

Names and Labels Are Deceptions

Names are useful in that they help you know who someone's talking to. But they can also be a deception because the truth is, we're all the same, we're all one. Who you are, who you think you are, the personality you've constructed and the labels other people put on you — your name, your class, religion, sexuality, gender, nationality or something else —the physical body is your house. You are the inhabitant. You are the life force energy, the conscious awareness, the animating energy that makes us who we are instead of lifeless meat bags. When that energy leaves the body, we know our loved ones are really gone.

There is no physical part of the brain or body that science has found that is responsible for consciousness. This is because we are like light bulbs, shining light through these bodies.

The energy comes through us, and scientists will never find the source of that energy because it is not inside us. And while the light may go out, the source of that energy is the source of this entire universe, and it is infinite and eternal.

When we focus on these labels and identify with our temporary experience, we mistake our deepest sense of self for some temporary experience. We'll even see other people as labels instead of infinite beings of potential, and it allows for the dehumanization of each other.

Labels and classifications are essential for efficient communication. It's the mistaking of these labels for the actual thing that gets us into trouble. When people and objects become labels, symbols, ideas and conceptual representations in our mind, we can no longer take in the beingness or essence of what we are observing.

For example, most people when asked who they are would say their name (of course, it would be very strange and unhelpful to say "God" or "consciousness"), but we would be wise to remember we are so much more.

When a tree becomes the word "tree," we reduce it down to four little letters and we forget to admire it.

Truly looking at trees and marveling at the complexity and beauty in every leaf and branch and vein, feeling the bark and taking in the essence of the tree, this is a spiritual experience.

When we live in labels and thoughts, we may not even

notice the tree, and we will miss out on the beauty of it and the feeling of gratitude for its air, wood, and shade. These miraculous trees feed us, shelter and warm us.

And there's not one tree that's bad, a failure, or stupid in my book. Are humans any less deserving of such grace because some of them may have grown up in harsh environments or without enough nourishment?

Whether it's people or trees, we create labels for them. If we're not mindful, we'll mentally replace the people with their label — good, bad, mean, nice, stupid, smart, etc...

When we do this, we feel disconnected from everyone around us, and ourselves. Loneliness, fear, greed, jealousy, anger and hatred all arise when we feel we're on our own and we better look out for ourselves (which is not as effective a strategy as teamwork and building big things through cooperation and mutual benefit).

When we can appreciate the essence of something, we can truly see it for what it is. We'll look up and look people in the eyes, we'll love and appreciate every plant and insect, we'll let them be as they are and not as we project, and that is paying the highest respect we possibly can.

Truly honoring the life in another being, rather than creating a fake relationship with a false label in your mind, is the greatest gift we can give.

This is how we let them in, this is how they let us in, and a merging takes place. Through them we see ourselves, and through us they see themselves.

This is the universe's highest level of beings — humans — experiencing themselves through each other, in full HD 4k picture with surround sound. People pay good money for

TVs that aren't even as good as our eyes and ears. It'd be a shame if we failed to take in every detail.

When we can see the life and humanity in everyone, all cruelty would cease immediately. We would see that we are all one, life seeing life, instead of egos seeing egos. We would be overcome with love through this deep connection and understanding.

There is so much to be grateful for. There's so much goodness in the world. To not focus on that would be to miss out on the beauty of our lives.

Usually, we think that our thoughts are determined by the things that happen in our life — if good things happen, we'll think happy thoughts. But good and bad only exist in our mind.

The universe isn't good or bad. Like quantum mechanics shows, it exists in all states at once, a wave of probability, and our level of awareness determines the quality of our experience.

Whether we realize it or not, we choose how we see the world. The universe is everything, and so it is whatever we make it out to be.

As we know, matter acts as a wave of energy until consciousness observes it. This is the consciousness of the universe interacting with the consciousness of life on this planet. Everything you see is consciousness looking back at you. If you believe the universe is bad, it is. If you believe it's good, it is. So how do we form the best, most beneficial beliefs that won't lead us into a cult or some other delusion?

Some people think we have to believe what we were born into. For most of the world, if your parents are Christian, you'll be a Christian. If your parents are Hindu, you'll be a Hindu. We're all born into some system of beliefs, whether it's religious, atheistic, scientific or optimistic.

But something I've learned is that we can create our own beliefs. We can choose them, make new original ones, borrow bits from some, and discard parts from others. It's not something you have to be convinced about. It's not something that you're either born believing or you don't, it's truly a choice.

We can choose self-limiting beliefs, or we can choose to believe we're capable of anything. We can choose to believe that our body is weak and can't heal, or we can choose to believe that we can overcome and heal from anything. It's completely in our hands, and some beliefs can bring about real, positive changes in our lives.

Another thing to remember is, we can't truly own anything. We don't even own these bodies. We may inhabit them, but we didn't do anything to acquire them, earn them, buy them or build them.

And no more can someone own the sky than own the land or anything else. There may be a piece of paper that says you own it, there may be objects you keep behind a fence or behind a locked door or in a locked safe, but you don't own them in any real sense.

We are all nothing more than temporary stewards of this stuff, custodians. In a hundred years, someone else will be using all your precious stuff.

Native Americans understood that the Earth's land is here for all to enjoy. Buddhist philosophy calls this nonattachment. From these beliefs, a mutual responsibility for the Earth and all of its inhabitants is developed. And this is how we will build a better future for ourselves and our offspring. So even though we say "my body" and "my house," it's important to remember that while these labels can be useful for communication, they can also impair us from seeing the deeper truth.

We Are More Than Labels

Space, silence, and our pure conscious awareness are similar in that nothing can alter those states. You can never freeze space, burn space, or altar space in any way. It's eternal and unchanging. This is the nature of our true selves.

Misidentification with our temporary experience mistakes our deepest sense of self for our passing thoughts and ever changing concepts about ourself. We are not labels, and **any attempt to label us divides, disconnects and distracts us.**

For example, Christianity's concept of love; Hinduism's concepts of living an honest, non-violent life that doesn't harm others; Judaism's teachings of fairness, justice and forgiveness; Islam's teachings of charity and community; and Buddhism's lessons on compassion; are all the same at their core.

It's a shame we put so much attention on labels — God, Allah, Adonai, Ram, Zeus, Mother Nature. There is absolutely no reason these separate faiths have to remain separate. We don't have to divide the world into different religions or cultures or races or genders, because we're all conscious awareness, with no gender, race, culture, religion or belief system. We can and should still honor our differences, love and cherish all of the beautiful expressions of the human spirit. Every single culture is beautiful and insightful. But when we focus solely on differences and labels, and we identify with them, then we lose touch with the divine and sacred inside all of us.

When we live in Label Land, it's easy to write people off. We'll disregard people's opinions based on where they're from or what group they belong to.

If someone makes a mistake or has a bad day, we may misjudge a person as "bad." But humans are too complex and have too much potential to be reduced down to a few labels.

People tell me I'm a white man, and I am aware that my appearance would put me into a binary category of white as opposed to color, and man as opposed to woman. But I don't identify as those. It may be helpful to use those labels when trying to describe me in a crowd of people, but that is not how I identify. I just am.

Our sense of self is merely the turning of our consciousness back onto itself so that it can experience itself. This is how we can know ourselves — our true selves, our essence.

When we look for ourselves, and we peer through the thoughts, the sense-objects, and the physical body, what remains must be our true self. It can't be a delusion because you are merely observing without placing any labels, opinions or judgments. In fact, it is these labels, opinions and judgments that obscure our view in the first place.

How to See the World Without Labels

Once we realize that we are framing our reality, then we can learn how to reframe the way we see stressful situations, and we can look beyond the conditioned mind's way of seeing things.

There is a Buddhist concept called emptiness. This concept is about how reality is an illusion. We tend to believe we're seeing reality as it truly is, but if we dig a little deeper, if we spend a little time actually inspecting this illusion, what we find is that we are only seeing our interpretation of reality — a projection of our beliefs, our identity, and our concept of reality. We are not seeing the actual truth of what is taking place around us and within us.

When we are constantly labeling and judging things, we create a filter between ourselves and the world.

So we get sucked into these dramas with our mental story as it bumps up against someone else's mental story. The truth gets lost in the process because of the fundamental misperception that everything exists independently and inherently on its own.

Whereas we know with closer inspection that everything only exists in an interdependent reality. Everything exists because of the causes and effects that came before it. There is no solidity, no permanence and no separateness, even though we mistakenly think there is.

For example, we tend to think that who we are — the self — is made up of the mind and body. But the mind and the body are two separate things.

There is only one self though, which means that the true "I," that sense of self we all have, is either divided in two and thus a plural entity, which goes against how we experience this life.

Are we the mind then? All we have to do is look at the ever changing nature of our mind to find the answer. Our thoughts are constantly arising and falling away, sense perceptions are constantly arising within our consciousness and falling away, and our emotions are constantly changing, yet we remain. So we cannot be the mind.

Are we our body, in which our cells are constantly being born and dying? We are in a constant state of death and rebirth.

No cell in our body will still be there in a few years. We will soon, physically, be an entirely new person, and yet the self remains the same, the stream of consciousness unbroken and unchanged.

So the self cannot be found in our body either. We can keep looking forever, but we will not find a person sitting at the captain's chair in our brain.

The reason we look within to discover the empty nature of our existence is because this is where our consciousness has the most access to.

Once we develop an understanding that there is no "me," no independent inherent self, then the emptiness of the universe becomes self-evident, and all of the artificial concepts we project become clear.

Emptiness is not a negative concept that states that nothing exists or that nothing matters. Far from it. It simply reminds us that the things we get happy or sad about are both illusions, so we can enjoy the good and not stress the bad.

Once we recognize the emptiness within ourselves, we can see it all around us.

We can see that a table is not a table. A table is a concept we put on an object because of its form and function. Yet, if you look closely, there is no table. If you were to take sandpaper and sand down a table until all that remains is a little stub from one of the table legs, you wouldn't be able to point to one moment where it lost its essence of tableness. Does a table need legs in our imagined concept of a table? Can three legs work? What if the table is cut in half, do we have two tables or no table? As we can see, there is no inherent table that can be found in the form.

If it's the function that makes a table, then the floor could be a table because we can put plates and cups on it. But that is not what a floor really is. Just because a horse and a car get us where we want to go, doesn't make them the same thing.

Eventually, what we come to realize is that there is no table within the table. There is no essence of a table that exists inherently.

It is simply a collection of parts that humans call a table and use as a table. But those parts are made of tinier parts which are ultimately nothing more than vibrating energy projecting an illusion.

The table only existed in an interdependent relationship between the witness and the object. Once we move beyond this illusory subject/object reality, we stop being separate from the universe and we start becoming one with it.

So once we develop a deep sense of the truth about our existence, that **we are the creator and witness simultaneously,** we begin to understand that nothing is actually as it seems.

Any mental story about any situation, object, or personal identity, is merely part of the projection and not to be taken as absolute fact.

So let's stop getting sucked into the fake drama and caught up in labels and identities. Let's notice those labels like inconvenient, boring, sucks, and all of the other ones we say to ourselves that make us suffer.

Notice any mental turmoil and the displeasing situations that sparked it, and see them both as the interdependent, constantly changing, cause-and-effect playing out before our eyes.

All the meaning, all of the clinging on and attachment to certain situations, possessions, or even ego and identity, dissolve once we simply recognize that they don't exist inherently on their own, permanent, as we perceive them. We can practice this in our daily life by reminding ourselves that whatever is consuming our thoughts is merely a fabrication — a fictional story we are telling ourselves — and we don't have to believe in it. We don't have to invest in it. We can simply allow everything to come and go as the universe intended, in its infinite perfection and infinite wisdom, so nothing can shake us from our deeply rooted center of peace.

Life Lesson 14

We Are One With the Universe

If you were to look at human skin under an electron microscope, you would not be able to tell where the human being begins and ends. There is no fine barrier between the person and the universe, there is a gradual flow from one to the next. The only reason we perceive separateness is because of the limitations of our senses.

Human beings can only see 0.00035 percent of the electromagnetic light spectrum. We can only hear .000004 percent of the sound spectrum. If we could see infrared, ultraviolet, x-rays and gamma rays, and if we could hear the whole spectrum of sounds, our universe would appear very differently. There would be no empty space. It would be so full that all we could see would be a sea of energy, and the oneness of everything would become clear

There is no separate you, no separateness at all, despite what may appear to our limited eyes. There's only a deep interconnectedness. This separateness, this solid reality, is an illusion. It might not even exist at all.

Illusion of Separateness

Every atom is mostly empty space. If the matter of an atom, the nucleus, was the size of a peanut, the empty space of that atom would be the size of a baseball stadium.

If all the empty space was taken out of the human body, all of the matter left over — the atomic and subatomic particles — could fit within the size of a speck of dust. If you took out the empty space of every human being, the matter left over from every human being could fit into the size of a sugar cube.

The matter that we see — all the objects that we perceive as physical structure — is an illusion. They are energetic atoms that signal to our brains something is there. Our brains are like these radio receivers, picking up a signal of energy (through our senses) and reconstructing that into a three dimensional picture.

But in reality, there is no solidity. These atoms are flying around, vibrating, creating vibrational frequencies, like radio waves, that our brain receives and then projects as brain waves to our consciousness as a recreated simulation of the world around us.

When we look even closer into the stuff that makes up

stuff — the particles that make up atoms — there might not even be any matter at all.

Today, the common assumption made by physicists is that the elementary particles that make up everything are infinitely small, massless points of concentrated energy. Only when elementary particles interact with another elementary particle, the Higgs boson — also known as the God particle — do they take on the appearance of having mass.

So everything we see is a well-constructed illusion, a virtual reality that appears real and takes a significant amount of importance in our lives, but still no matter what is never worth getting upset over.

As we know, when no one is looking at these particles, they turn back into waves of energy and probability, but in reality, that's all there is.

Only the appearance of matter is seen by us, not actual matter. And so a clearer model of our universe would be to see it as a universal field of consciousness creating separate points of consciousness which collapse into the illusion of a solid object when an interaction between consciousnesses takes place.

So whenever anything happens that we get so upset about, we're falling for the illusion.

It's like dreams. No matter how crazy they are, we always fall for it. We always believe it's real until the moment we wake up (unless we train ourselves to recognize dreams the way lucid dreamers do). And then we say, "Wow, that was crazy. I can't believe I fell for that."

Even if I dreamt I was in China, and I knew I went to bed in New York, I'd still fall for the illusion. Even if I was flying through the sky, I would be positive that it was real until I woke up. Our brains are wired to believe the illusion because it's a survival mechanism. We need to eat food, and so it's better if our brains block out all of the irrelevant information so we can focus on survival. But even ancient humans recognized that there was a deeper reality beyond what we can see and hear.

It's when we think the stuff is all there is, that we suffer so much when we lose our stuff, crave other people's stuff, and hate displeasing stuff.

There is no doubt that this is a great illusion, but we're still living in a simulation within our mind. If we were dogs, we'd live in a different simulation, more monochromatic and the world would be more alive with smells and sounds.

Fish don't realize there is water. It took humans a long time to realize there was air, and we still don't fully realize we're in a sea of energy, connected with everything, manifesting/projecting/cocreating an illusory interpretation of reality.

We think we're separate but we are intricately connected to all matter and energy. The prefix of universe, uni, means one, and there is only oneness in the entire universe — this planet, the sun, Jupiter, the Milky Way, and every single galaxy and atom are inextricably linked, forever entangled in this quantum universe.

You are connected to everything. You are not separate from anyone or anything. Everyone is you and you are everyone. Star dust, as if by miracle, arranged itself into all of us. The universe is conscious because there is consciousness in the universe. You are an essential part of this universe and vital to its unfolding evolution.

To experience this oneness, one need only close their eyes and turn their attention inward, towards the vast infinite space of pure conscious being, where the loneliness and separateness of the material illusion cease to exist.

The more peace and happiness we have, the greater our capacity for love — not romantic love, but love for all of life. The more we meditate, the more our mind can rest and we can move beyond thinking and into a state of conscious awareness. As our consciousness rises and expands, our unconscious behavior, choices, addictions, impulses, poor decisions, and habitual thinking diminishes. Our intentions, thoughts and actions come into alignment and any inner conflict evaporates. We bring a sense of wholeness to ourselves. Who we want to be and who we are become one.

Everything Is One

The sensing of separateness comes down to us labeling and viewing things as different and separate. Upon both closer inspection and a broadening of our perspective, we can see how things are related and connected. We can see that every living being shares a distant ancestor in the tree of life. We are all one.

All life is connected.

We are connected to the trees whose air we breathe, the sun that sustains us, and all of the universe of which we are a part. We are all energy swimming in a sea of energy, like how a drop of water in the ocean is still the ocean.

The energy that animates me is the same energy that animates you.

It is the same energy that animates all life on this planet. It has been passed onto each of us ever since the first single-celled organism came into being. The more you look past people's physical surface, the more you will see the oneness in all living things. We all have an inexplicable drive to live, to love, and to be loved. Every animal – and even plants we're now learning – strive to live, take care of their young, and live in balance with each other. Generosity, kindness, cooperation and compassion are survival mechanisms we each possess and can help us in witnessing the oneness of this universe.

We are the trees because we breathe their air. We are the earth because we eat its fruits. We are the stars of which we're made. When we pay as much attention to how things are connected and interdependent, as we do to the things themselves, a deep sense of oneness arises. Only 14 billion years ago, everything in the universe was in a single point of space.

Not everyone is able to see and understand the relationships and connections around us. We all notice different things because there are many varying degrees of consciousness. At lower levels of consciousness, we tend to fixate on physical objects, and even people appear as objects. The more conscious we become, the higher state of awareness. We're able to see non-material things, like relationships, patterns and connections. We see how all things affect each other, we see the embers from the past bruning in the present, and we see how the seeds we plant today will blossom in the future.

At low levels, everything appears separate, isolated, alone, random and chaotic. At high levels, oneness, beauty and meaning emerge. Low levels are states of fear, anger and greed. High levels are ones of love, compassion and gratitude.

In Buddhism, they meditate on interconnectedness —

how all things are related. As we grow more conscious, we'll see that the only thing that matters is our relationship with everything around us, not the stuff. For example, if I see a chocolate cake and I am in a wise, conscious relationship with it, I will notice my craving, notice my future sadness if I eat the whole thing, and I will instead either take a bite or peacefully decline. In a relationship of ignorance, I will become overcome with desire, I will only be able to think about immediate gratification, and I will gorge myself until I am sick.

Turning Separateness into Oneness

Our bodies were not designed to see the reality. They were designed to see food, water, potential mates and potential dangers. This is the illusion that most of us live in. But through closer inspection, we can see the inseparability of it all.

This is why ancient tribes worshiped the sun, because they understood the connection between the sun and all living things on Earth. They worshiped the tree, the wind, the soil, and the rain for the same reasons.

If a table were floating in space, and there was nothing around it, we would not know how big it was, if it was right side up or upside down, unless something else was next to it.

This shows us that nothing exists on its own. Everything exists in relation to everything around it. A dollar isn't much money today, but it was a lot of money two hundred years ago. Relationship is everything.

Relationships and connections are more important than any object itself.

Once you put a person next to that table floating in space,

we can start to see how big it is, we can start to see if it's right side up or upside down or sideways. As we put more things nearby, we begin to have an even clearer picture.

Everything in the universe behaves this way. Remember those infinitely small particles that have no mass? Only when we collide them into each other can we see how they react with something else. All of a sudden, it has the traits of mass.

This concept encapsulates Einstein's theory of relativity, because everything can only have characteristics relative to the things around it. I would win a foot race against a bunch of 2-year-olds, but I would come in dead last at the Olympics.

The nonmaterial, nonphysical relationship between objects is the only thing that's real. Object and subject combined is what brings our entire universe into existence. From nonduality, the delusion of duality emerges. When we understand that things are not how they appear, oneness can be seen.

Even the image we have of ourselves is an illusion, no different than the illusion of a table.

For example, we may say a person has beautiful hair, but after that person gets a haircut, we don't admire the chopped off hair lying on the floor. I doubt anyone has looked at the floor of a salon and thought, "That is beautiful hair."

Beauty arises from the overall wholistic relationship between a person, their hair, and the other person who witnessed it. When we look deeply into the universe, we find our own consciousness at the center of it. We see that nothing exists independently of anything else. And we see that we are the ones creating the meaning and illusion.

Once we do enough self-examination and realize there is

no self to be discovered, that there is no physical nor nonphysical component that can be determined to be the self, we can start to see the entire universe in this way. We can start to recognize the interdependent nature of all phenomena, instead of the illusion of inherent existence, as the Buddhists call it. Inherent existence is the misperception that things exist separately and independent of all other phenomena.

So, simply meditating on this fact that everything we experience is a fictional, conceptual framework to understand the world — as we were programmed to do so we can find food, avoid danger, and reproduce as the biological organisms that we are — helps us realize the oneness all around us.

That connection, the taking in of the world and projecting our worldview back out, creates a oneness within us and around us. Seeing the causes and effects that led to this moment gives us a truer way of seeing the world. And it is a unifying, peaceful way of seeing the world. There is nothing that can disturb our inner peace since nothing that happens is inherently existing. When we recognize the mental constructs, and our own role as their creators, a deep peace and joy can be felt, and a liberation from those concepts of division occurs.

Life Lesson 15

Aloneness is Not Same
as Loneliness

There is no separate you, no separateness at all. There's only deep interconnectedness. There's only oneness. The difference between loneliness and aloneness is that loneliness is when being alone causes suffering. Aloneness is ultimately recognizing others as yourself, when you realize that you are one with everything.

For people out there who have no one to talk to, I get it. We live in a world where people have to pay doctors to listen to them talk for an hour. But trust me, there are people out there like you who feel the same. If all these people can get together, then everyone will have someone to talk to and someone who will listen. We need to get back to a place where people can talk to each other, where we don't need to pay strangers. It's very healing.

It takes a little courage to put yourself out there, but you will find people who are receptive to real connections and authentic conversations, instead of making small talk about the weather and other pleasantries.

The internet, for all its flaws, is also a great place to find people in real life to talk to, people who share your interests and share your desire for meaningful relationships. There are a lot of groups online that meetup offline, and communities built around shared interests like hiking or spirituality. There are strong, welcoming communities out there, and if there's not one in your neighborhood, give starting one a try.

But no matter how packed or empty our social calendar is, in between the social visits spirituality can erase that longing. With spirituality and meditation, we can create immense peace in our aloneness so that it's not lonely.

Human connection is important, but with a rich inner spirit, it doesn't become a burden to be alone. It becomes a peaceful respite from the chaotic, turbulent, busy lives so many of us lead.

To talk to someone also means listening — a spiritual practice in itself. This is to be truly present with someone, not in our own head, but letting them come into ours.

They say the best conversationalists are the best listeners, and I think that has a lot of truth to it. The more interest you take in someone else, the better conversations you have. The more you focus on others, the less self-consciousness, insecurity and anxiety there is.

One of the best and easiest ways to get through a dark time is by taking an interest in someone else. When we focus on helping others, our own mental state and inner monologue become secondary and unimportant. Our ego dissolves and all unhappiness drifts from our awareness.

It's counterintuitive, but when we obsess about our own happiness, we suffer; when we focus on others' happiness, we become happy.

When we do the talking, we share what we already know. While it is healing to let out our thoughts so we can process and move on from them, and feeling heard is healing; the real power lies in listening, learning, helping someone else heal.

Listening helps others heal. And by helping others, we help ourself the most.

I love living in this world where selflessness is the most selfish thing we can do. Thank God for that, or else the world would be a much scarier place. So try this ancient spiritual practice of listening. Listen to others, listen to your own thoughts, and most of all listen to your heart — the intuition, instincts and feelings.

Dealing with Loneliness

There is no doubt about it, we are social creatures. Isolation is a punishment far worse than even a violent and dangerous prison. In the old days, exile from the kingdom was considered worse than death, and often meant a brutal death due to the harsh living conditions.

We humans need connection because we are a deeply interconnected species in an interconnected universe. We depend on one another. We need others like we need fresh air and sunshine. Unfortunately, we are living in an ever-increasingly isolated society. Day-by-day we become more alone and disconnected, and this is not natural for humans.

However, there are things we can do when we are deprived of physical touch. There are ways to diminish the suffering that our lack of connection causes. We can tap into that inner joy and peace we all have inside of us that is not dependent on any external circumstance or experience.

People have physical needs. We have these material bodies and we need food to eat, water to drink, shelter and security. But we are spiritual beings and we need love and compassion as well.

We are social mammals who are only here today because we survived by living in very closely connected tribes. Today, our communities have changed but human touch is still a need. While the internet has people looking more at their screens and less at each other, it can also be a very powerful tool for creating deep connections offline.

Even though the way we connect has changed, there are still invaluable opportunities for connection all around us. There's small talk with our neighbors and store clerks, which can create a measurable change in our mood and day. We can still make new friends and find new social experiences. Many places today are offering social events for people to connect. If we find all of these available options unsatisfactory, we may need to turn inward and examine the nature of our internal voice. Is it too judgmental? Does it have too high expectations? Often our own fear and beliefs are our greatest obstacle.

Some people though, despite their efforts, are truly alone.

Many people have no way of interacting with people. Some are in prison, and often at no fault of their own. Others may be in a hospital or under nursing care. For these people, and for all of us who are feeling more disconnected in an ever increasingly isolated society, the human daily requirement for social connection is not being met.

In these cases, the suffering we experience from loneliness can only be resolved in the spiritual dimension, where we can find that source of love that connects us to everything else in the universe.

Monks, gurus, mystics, saints and sadhus have discovered infinite bliss in total solitude for millennia, and this skill is a birthright for every human. The more time we have alone, the more time we have to meditate.

Just as we can feel lonely in a crowd, so too, the oneness of the universe can seem lonely. When you realize that everywhere you look is you looking back at yourself, that all there is is one, we realize we are alone.

While this may seem scary at first, it liberates us to feel safe, secure and connected at all times because the entire universe is inside of us, all our ancestors and all future generations as well.

While human-to-human connection feels wonderful, the deeper connection happens within. We are not these meat suits.

When someone we love dies, we don't keep their body, sit it at the dinner table and pretend that it's still the person that we loved. We understand deep down that who they are has left and is no longer there. It is in the nonphysical where the spiritual dimension lies, and that nothing is everything.

When we tap into the energy of universal love within, we tap into oneness, inseparable from every living being and the rest of the universe. This nonmaterial dimension, which we have access to simply by closing our eyes and turning our attention inward, is peace, joy, and oneness.

As we become familiar with this space, loneliness disappears. Worries and sadness melt away. **Darkness cannot survive the light.**

Oftentimes, the lonelier we are, the easier it is to tap into that infinite spiritual reservoir of love within.

We don't need any person or being or object to receive our love at higher states of consciousness because we are in love with love itself, with life, the universe, and everything that is made up of this universal loving energy. Nowhere is cut off from the universe. That love pervades all.

Whether it's a cat, a puppy, a romantic love interest, or even a chair, we can show it the same level of gratitude and love. We can fill ourselves with love and gratitude for anything that we experience in our lives.

We only pet dogs and cats because they show us their love and appreciation. But when we sense that alive loving energy from the universe all around us, we feel the loving grace of the universe coming back to us. To give love is to feel love.

And the **universe is love.** Its loving embrace is accessible to every single one of us — religious and nonreligious.

There is a massive amount of energy in every single atom. It holds the atom together, holds molecules together, and makes up everything. It is love that holds planets and stars together in a loving embrace, dancing for eternity. The energy that made everything — that is eternal and omnipresent — is love.

But when we look at this energy, this aliveness that animates our bodies and that we sense in all of nature and everything in the universe, in every single atom, is the great mystery for us to ponder endlessly. It is a miracle, this building block of our universe, fundamental and foundational, that our greatest scientists are only beginning to understand.

By closing our eyes and spending a few moments not doing but being, we can touch this peace and oneness. When we touch it and become familiar with it, we can sense it in every moment of every day. We'll always be able to rely on it, and very soon contentment, fulfillment and gratitude will predominate our lives.

Every breath we take means we have the potential to touch that peaceful ocean within. Every inhale, like the waves coming in. Every exhale, the waves coming out. We allow the oceanic quality of our breath to relax us, no differently than the real ocean does, as we bask in the sea of tranquility.

We Are All One. We Are Never Alone.

When we operate from our ego, we have a very small, narrow perspective. By looking at things from a broader perspective, from other people's perspective, or even from the universal perspective, a much greater wisdom can arise within us.

Only through meditation and mindfulness can we truly see things from the broadest perspective possible. We no longer make ourselves the victim because we don't frame situations as "happening to me." We don't compare our possessions with someone else who has more. Instead, we simply watch the play of life unfold, delighting in all of the drama and comedy alike. This is the secret to living a joyful, peaceful life.

The normal way we go about our daily lives is to perceive everything as happening to us, but what really happens to us? In reality, things just happen around us. Maybe even something happens to these bodies of ours, but that's not us.

Our point of consciousness shines its light out onto the world, and we have a perspective of being at the center of the universe — illusion.

Our brains tell us we're these bodies so that they can control us, and it works. Now we believe the ego is us, we believe every word it says, and it starts comparing ourselves and our circumstances to everyone else.

In yoga and meditation, or whenever we give ourselves the time to close our eyes and sit in stillness and quiet, we're able to shut off all that grasping mind.

As we turn our senses inward, we're able to simply be and experience the interconnectedness of all things and beings.

In our normal mode of thinking, we could be jealous of our neighbor's new boat. In higher consciousness, we appreciate what we have.

In our normal mode of thinking, we compare our looks to others — those around us, in the billboards, the magazines and the movies. In mindfulness, we appreciate life itself, and we're grateful for our wisdom, compassion, intuition, and we appreciate that same beauty and inner nature of others.

We don't compare. There's no jealousy. We simply see and appreciate the beauty in the world. As we expand our perspective to the entire universe, loneliness disappears, rivalries dissolve and only love remains. We are living in the most remarkable living painting. The night sky, the variety of flowers, and the daily sunrises and sunsets, all free gifts from a stunning artist. Life is a canvas. What will you paint?

Love for all is love for yourself.

I truly wish for everyone to get all the love they deserve and more. But even for myself, I often do not feel love reciprocated from people who I've shown love to. I feel, as anyone else, that people are not always as loving or kind as I wish them to be. But, when we do not get the love we deserve, we can always give love to someone else — and that is a form of self-love.

Once we find oneness — the true nature of reality — our expanded perspective suddenly finds petty squabbles meaningless. Minor stresses become insignificant and social anxieties disappear because all there is love and compassion.

The self dissolves and dissipates, becoming an energetic field that radiates throughout the entire universe, formless and boundaryless.

When we have a universe-size perspective, what else could possibly matter to us compared to the sheer beauty and size of this universe, or compared to the majesty and magic of life itself? What daily little inconvenience or annoyance, or traffic or bad boss, can hold a candle to the infinite eternal awesomeness of the universe?

So whenever we get bogged down in the day-to-day issues and difficulties, all we have to do is remember, think about, and focus on this incredible miracle of existence. It is a miracle that the infinite number of things that had to happen for me to be here writing this and for you to be there reading it, were able to happen in precisely the right way.

We are but tiny specks on a planet, which is a tiny speck in the solar system, which is a tiny speck in the galaxy, which is a tiny tiny speck in the universe.

Like ants on an anthill, building their cities, living their lives, doing what is important to them at the moment, without falling for the trick that they are the center of the universe. They care not about their legacy nor how much they can achieve and acquire before they die. Are we not as deserving as ants to be free from anxiety, fear and stress?

Our lives are no more important than the ants, and yet no less important than anyone else's.

Life is life. It's all connected and it's all essential to the greater whole. A tiger doesn't eat a gazelle; it is simply life becoming life.

Death is never the end. It is only the process of rebirth. This is what we see when our consciousness expands to relationships.

Everywhere we look, everything around us and within us, is a miracle that we take for granted. The dance of life is playing out in all its beauty, exactly as it's supposed to. When we fixate on objects, we can't help but compare those objects to ourselves and our situations.

As we meditate, reflect and expand our consciousness, we notice how it all works together, the delicate inner workings, the relationships, and the energy coming from people, animals, plants, and everything around us. We feel connected to the sun which gives us life, and the moon for sustaining us. There's only gratitude and awe when we can see clearly.

This is why we must see beyond our perspectives, beyond

borders and cultures, beyond nations and races, and see the light of consciousness in others and ourselves as one.

When we expand our perspective, we don't lash out at other people. We recognize they have a life we don't know about. They have an inner life we're even less aware of. We don't know anyone's struggles. We don't know their trauma. All we know is, we would be them if we were in their shoes, we would do what they did, because we are all the same. Only our bodies and experiences differ.

Deep down, we all seek love, connection, joy, health and happiness. With an expanded perspective, we can value people's different opinions, we can forgive their mistakes, and we can relax into the knowledge that everyone is simply doing their best with where they are and what they have.

By expanding our consciousness, we can see how we can best lift people up, help them through any misfortune, and provide a space for them to be without being judged, criticized or dehumanized.

Too often, humans try to make situations better but only end up making them worse because we were operating from a place of fear or ego. When we quiet the mind, we can see the root causes beyond the symptoms, and this is how we can truly help others and ourselves.

Life Lesson 16

Suffering Exists in the Mind

All suffering exists in the mind. No matter what happens to you, no matter how terrible, there can be peace.

When I was in India walking down the street, I saw a guy in a shirt that said, "**Pain is mandatory, suffering is optional.**" Only in India do I see these profound spiritual shirts that blow my mind. That shirt touched on such a deep truth. Pain is a signal to the brain that makes sure we take our hand away from fire. But suffering happens when the mind says, "Fire bad. Pain bad."

There are no problems in the present moment. Problems

only exist as a mental reaction to something from the past or something that we imagine may happen in the future.

Being present is to realize the perfection of life, not as good or bad, but perfect exactly as it is, with no resistance, no aversion, and no judgments. Just peace and joy for life.

In Buddhism they say that all suffering is caused by either aversion to pain, or craving of pleasure. When something is perceived as undesirable, the mind starts to say, "This is bad. I don't want this." The negative thoughts spur on negative emotions, causing suffering. A tension arises between reality and what the mind desires.

On the flip side, things we perceive as pleasurable, that we have a strong craving and longing for, disturb our inner peace as well.

When we realize we have an internal source of peace, the "good" and "bad" stuff on the outside no longer hold so much importance. No matter what the external circumstance is, suffering ceases when we are peaceful.

If one link in a chain fails, the whole chain fails. So too is our cosmic web of existence. Everything is an essential interconnected part of this universe, part of the universal creation.

Like how an actor in a play is nothing without the writer, director, co-stars, lights and sound crew, costume designers and everything that goes into it; we are all part of the collective consciousness, inseparable from the whole. If we were to change one thing, the whole thing collapses.

We're all trying to find our role and purpose in life, and that journey of discovery *is* our role and purpose.

Understanding that all suffering happens in our mind is a strange concept to a lot of people. But I ask you then, Where else in the world is there suffering? In pain, which is no more than an electrical signal in our brain? Surely not. In the harsh words of others? The sound as it's traveling from someone's mouth to my ears has no suffering. Only when the words reach my brain, does my ego get bruised.

Suffering only exists in our mind as the anticipation of unfavorable events, desires that are unmet, or regrets from the past that still live on in the memories of our mind.

Stop Doing Things All the Time

A daily meditation practice is all you need for a calm life. Most people spend 100% of their waking life doing something — getting ready for work, going to work, working, going home, enjoying some entertainment, socializing, and pretty soon it's back to bed.

This constant doing disconnects us from our true state of peace — our balanced centeredness.

We live in the world of good and bad, ups and downs. In the middle of good and bad, and up and down, is our centered, peaceful state, which has no opposite. It's so important to spend a few minutes every day putting all our distractions away to sit still doing nothing.

When we can sit in peace and have moments of quieting our mind, impulsive decisions disappear from our life. As we bring peace into our life, even if it's for no more than a few minutes here and there throughout the day, everything we do becomes more peaceful.

Like training a muscle in the gym, we can train our mind to be a tool at our disposal instead of this unconscious thinking mechanism that does whatever it wants to do. Instead of generating suffering, it can generate joy. Instead of thinking random thoughts that pop into our head, we can think about the best moments of our life, and about the beauty and wonder in the present moment.

So meditation is like a workout for the mind, which I would say is the most important part of the body. We spend so many hours a week working out our body, or filling our head with knowledge (and sometimes junk).

And even though we spend almost no time working out our mind to generate more joy and less suffering, a few minutes a day can change our whole life.

Studies have shown that Buddhist monks have larger parts of the brain that are responsible for empathy, and smaller parts of the brain that are responsible for fear. These studies show that a few brief weeks of meditation can physically change the shape of our brain.

So I would say meditation for mental health is equally as important as taking care of our physical health. Perhaps even more so, because if we are not mentally well, we are not going to be able to take care of our body.

To date, there is no other practice known to science that reshapes our mind in such a profound way as meditation does.

It doesn't have to be the traditional sitting meditation either. Eckhart Tolle doesn't meditate, but he does stare out the window for hours a day, practicing presence and feeling the aliveness within.

What's important is that we bring some peace into our life, step back from the constant doing, and allow our mind to rest, reflect, introspect and be present. Focusing on anything in the present moment, whether it's the breath, a mantra, a candle or a flower, has countless benefits that are available to everyone.

No matter where you are, you can close your eyes and be aware of your thoughts, observing what the thoughts are, the nature of the thoughts, how they jump from one thought to another, how they come and go, and we can really look at what a thought is. Then, as you're observing your thoughts, notice how you're aware of your thoughts and focus on that awareness. That's our higher consciousness, our highest intelligence. It's beyond the mind. We are no longer the thinkers of thoughts. We are aware of the thoughts, aware of the thinking. So if we cannot be thoughts, we must be awareness.

Release That Stress

Fear is an evolutionary advantage to make sure we run away from tigers and don't get too close to the edge of a cliff. It's a survival mechanism that triggers our fight or flight response. The stress constricts our blood vessels, sending extra blood to our limbs for strength. A surge of adrenaline heightens our senses, and we're best prepared to defend our lives.

But in modern society, we get fear and anxiety all the time. For most of us, a subtle level of stress is always beneath the surface — about money, our kids, whatever the news is scaring us about, our uncertain future or our regrettable past. Not exactly situations that require us to beat somebody up or run away.

Very rarely in modern society are we ever in real danger, but we live in this constant state of stress, fear and anxiety. When we don't allow our body's emotional state to relax and recover from that rather toxic state, that's what actually creates depression.

If the human body is under a sustained amount of fear, anxiety or stress, and you're not fighting or flighting, then that adrenaline keeps building up, the blood supply to our vital organs and brain becomes too depleted, until we eventually enter a freeze state.

This is our body's third defense mechanism — playing dead. This is why people with depression often don't want to leave their bed.

This is why it's vital to always be aware of our stress levels, to allow ourselves the time to release that stress, to recognize our relative safety so we don't take on new stress, and to make releasing stress a constant practice so it never accumulates.

Human beings are energy consuming and energy expending machines. We naturally seek to expend as little energy as possible, and advertising companies use that human drive to sell us a quick fix for our stress. Whether it's a pill, alcohol, food, luxury goods, or the distracting lure of entertainment and social media, in the long run they only end up making us more anxious because they don't release that stress, they only help us avoid it, repress it, or stuff it down further.

We have to do two things in order to fully heal from stress, because stress is both physical and mental.

First, we have to burn off that adrenaline. After a polar bear gets in a violent fight, it will go off and shake uncontrollably on the ground for a few minutes in order to raise its body temperature and move that adrenaline through its system. After that, it's totally fine, as if nothing ever happened. Human beings are not too different. Walking, running, jumping, dancing and lifting all help us process stressful events and they are essential to our wellbeing.

The second thing we need to do to get to the root of our anxiety is to allow our mind and body to reach a deep state of relaxation, rest and rejuvenation.

To do this, we have to turn our attention inwards. The best way for that to happen, according to me and science, is through meditation.

Facing those scary thoughts head on without distraction is the best way we can consciously release that stress, anxiety and fear.

There are no problems in the deep peace of pure conscious awareness. By closing our eyes and turning off the movie of our lives for a few minutes, we can recognize that it is nothing more than a movie, that we're just watching it, witnessing these bodies we inhabit, witnessing the universe, sometimes watching a comedy, sometimes a tragedy, but we are always safe in the theater.

If you're thinking I'm crazy, allow me to make one more observation. Our brains broadcast brainwaves, much like radio waves that can broadcast a TV signal. Those waves contain our thoughts and experience.

Stephen Hawking, after he lost the ability to control his body, had a microchip installed in his glasses that could read his thoughts and convert them to letters and words which could be spoken by a machine. Our bodies and minds are broadcasting an experience to our consciousness that is not of this physical dimension.

This is why our senses can be diminished, but our

consciousness can never be hurt, damaged, bruised, killed or altered in any way.

Only when we forget our true selves do we feel like we're inside the movie. That is what truly gives rise to our stress and worries. It can be hard to see at first because we can't turn around and see the film projector at the back of the cinema.

But the more we realize that we are the light bulb in the projector bringing life to the whole illusion, no moment or scene can disturb our inner peace.

All it takes is a little practice meditating on who we really are, remembering that this too will pass, that we'll be okay no matter what, and that there is nothing to fear because we know that the peace and joy we seek can always be found within.

Enlightenment isn't about not having dark days; it's about knowing how to process the dark times.

Enlightenment is not about never feeling sad. It's about knowing how to get through the sadness, and having a deeper understanding that all these emotions are temporary. It's knowing that while we're concerned, there's nothing to be concerned about. While we're sad, there's nothing to be sad about. We never have to be sad about being sad. We can watch the full spectrum of feelings and thoughts with peace, joy and love.

A witness can remain peaceful, even if witnessing chaos. We can remain peaceful, despite witnessing our own turbulent emotions. And that **inner peace is the antidote to inner chaos.**

There are a lot of people I meet who tell me they have

some problem in their life. They don't like something about the way their life is. They want to get away and they make a big decision to move or quit their job they hate, only to find wherever they move to, they're still there. Their new situations become identical to what they left. They still hate their new job because they would hate any job.

It wasn't the job or city they hated, it was their outlook and judgments that would make them habitually hate whatever was in front of them.

We probably all know someone like this, who is very negative and hates everything. They can even have a perfect dream life on paper, but the weather will always be either too hot or too cold. It's always the city they're in, the people in front of them, or the things around them that are the problem — never themselves.

When they leave a city to move to another city, they create the same situation because our mind projects our reality. We think we take in the external world to view it, but in reality we view what the mind projects.

The external world comes into our brain, then our brain analyzes it and creates a simulation of what we're perceiving, filtered through our mind's lens. **Unless you change, nothing changes.**

The narration of a film plays no small role. It sets the tone and tells us how we should feel about everything taking place. A caption is almost always more important than a photo because it frames the situation.

If we move cities, it can be because of hate, or love for a new place. How we think and feel about it determines the quality of our life, not the physical location. In just about any spot on Earth, someone has found a way to be happy there.

When I left New York for India, I loved my job, I loved my life. I wasn't running away from anything, but I thought that I could do more for the world and I thought that there was more to life than advertising and the hustle and bustle of New York City. It was born out of an excitement and curiosity for exploration and adventure. And that was exactly what I found. If I was trying to escape something, I would only be trying in vain to get away from myself.

I know that life can be difficult and hard. Sometimes it can be almost impossible to see the beauty in life, but it is there even in those darkest moments. There is still love and purpose and a reason to live for everybody, no matter who you are. We all have a gift to share with the world. If it's hard to find, keep looking. Like Albert Einstein said about struggling with problems, "Look deeper into nature, and then you will understand everything better."

Staying Present When You Want to Escape Present Moment

We've probably all heard about the peaceful quality of being in the present moment. But what about when the present moment is not so great? If the present moment is bad, isn't it better to relive our favorite memories or live in anticipation of our exciting future plans?

The truth is, there is nothing wrong with escaping into our favorite movie or some vacation getaway. The problem is when it happens compulsively. When we escape to avoid the present moment, when we escape due to fear, or when we escape to run away from our own feelings, we are letting problems fester and grow.

When we practice sitting with uncomfortable feelings,

uncomfortable situations, and making peace with whatever is happening in the here and now, we are training ourselves to trust ourselves — trust that we can face any adversity and overcome any challenge. This is Courage Training 101. Running away, even in our mind, only strengthens our fear. Staying in the moment is the practice of facing our fear, developing unshakable confidence, and increasing our capacity to handle difficult situations.

Whenever we're in a situation we desperately want to escape because we find it bad, unpleasant, and causing a lot of stress or anxiety, instead of looking away, look deeper. This is how we get to the core of our situation.

The closer we look at our problems, the more we'll see that there's no real problem there. And we realize that nothing can disturb our inner peace unless we allow it.

Once we look with calm eyes, we'll see the moment is actually not so unbearable, that we can handle it, we can accept it, and we'll see that there is nothing to worry about and nothing to stress about. We can still choose whether to walk away, stay, or try to change the situation, but we can do so without disturbing our inner peace or presence. However, if we are ever in a dangerous situation, it goes without saying that leaving and getting to physical safety is our first priority (spirituality does us little good if we're dead).

Nothing is worth our inner peace.

Life exists only in this constant stream of the present moment. In presence, we can take each moment as it comes, no matter what, and nothing can stop us. If we live in time — the past and future — we become lost, and we'll miss out on our brief, precious, wondrous life.

It's always the fear of something bad that is much worse than the actual bad thing. Fear builds up in our mind and we make the bad experience 10 times worse.

Even though the actual unpleasant experience may last a few seconds, we can live with that moment for days or weeks in advance, and for months or years after.

Even if we're escaping something bad for something good, we're training our mind to be afraid and look away. We have to look closer to realize that our suffering is not in any external object or situation, it's always within. It's always our fear, resistance and aversion that makes us suffer.

When we escape, either into our phone or substances or work or our own imagination, we are telling our subconscious mind that we are incapable of handling certain moments, that some experiences are too much for us to be present for. Pretty soon, we'll find even the slightest inconvenience overwhelming and unbearable.

But if we look closer, we'll see that it wasn't even so bad in the first place. Anyone that's scared of needles knows that it is the fear and anxiety leading up to the moment of pain that is a thousand times worse and much more traumatic than the brief little pinch of skin. The **suffering is much greater than the pain.**

Needles are tiny. Anxiety, stress and panic attacks make it big. A monk once told me, "Life always fires the first arrow. We usually fire a second arrow at ourselves — the arrow of anger, sadness and suffering. The key is to turn that first arrow into an acupuncture needle of healing."

He meant that when life sends us a struggle, it is always up to us how we respond, and we can turn any negative into something positive. **For every moment of life, we're either**

enjoying or we're growing.

The more we practice being present, deeply looking into our fears and worries and doubts, then we can bring some wisdom to these thoughts. Our negative thoughts that aren't serving us disappear as we consciously replace them with positive ones.

Training our mind to be present is training our mind to understand that this moment is good enough, and that there's nothing we need to escape.

We can still enjoy our favorite movies and TV shows, and we must still daydream and use our imaginations. But when it comes to escaping out of fear, boredom, or resistance to this moment, only by looking deeper can we truly heal, process what we're going through, and make a habit of being fully present, fully alive, fully alert in each moment, and fully at peace no matter what is happening around us.

There is no greater place to be than here. And there is no greater time to be there than now.

Don't Merely Accept Reality, Embrace It

When we are always thinking and always lost in thought, we are living in a prison of our own mind.

When we identify fully with our own thoughts, we become enslaved to any idea that pops into our head. It is like an all-powerful narrator lives inside our head and judges everything that happens as good or bad.

But the truth is, that narrator is our jailer. It is not who we truly are. The narrator keeps us from experiencing life as it is. It keeps us in a fantasy world where everything that happens is filtered through the lens of us staying in our prison and staying dependent on the narrator's false sense of security. It makes us believe that if we listen to our own fears, if we stay locked away, we'll stay safe.

We have to break free from the ego, we have to trust our instincts and intuition instead, and we have to live a life that is expansive and honest rather than small and scared.

That voice in our head, that mental narrative, is not the objective truth. It is the subjective opinion of a scared, jealous, negative, often immature entity whose only job is to search for danger — even when there is none.

When we attach ourselves to the story our mind tells us, we inevitably become locked in the prison of our own mind.

And we are the prison guard, we hold that prison door closed when we hold on to the stories of joy and happiness, success and desire, and we push that door closed with all of our might when we push up against any inconvenience, anything that is undesirable or displeasing.

To free ourselves from these mind-made prisons, we have to let go of the story in our head.

On some level, we think that the perfect life will free us. But it only takes a little bit of introspection and examination to recognize that there is no perfect life, that constant work is a natural part of life, and that every single person we know and love will get old and dissolve from this world.

On some level we think that if we stay in prison, we'll be able to build that perfect life of success, free from any kind of suffering. We believe the ego has our best interests at heart.

But we are living in a prison of dependency, built on a

fiction that our success will only go up, that our loved ones will stay the same age forever, that our lives will be conflict-free, and that there will be no suffering or setbacks.

So we have to open that door, let ourselves run free, let ourselves play and explore and go outside of that comfort zone and safety bubble we've caged ourselves inside of.

Because when we're playing, there is no suffering; there is only joy and curiosity. Anything that comes into our life can be another form of play.

Even a job loss can be seen as an exciting opportunity to play with what can come next. We can always ask ourselves, "What can this new adventure bring?"

In every situation, we can either look at it as going against our predetermined fictional idea of what life should be, or we can look at it as bringing in new discovery, new wonder and new opportunities.

The only difference is whether we are living in the mental prison of polarities and duality, where we categorize everything into good or bad, and where we are constantly in turmoil between the two. Or, we can get out of our prison cells and embrace everything, enjoying our life without attachment to any preconceived notions.

We can simply allow for everything that comes into our life to come, for however long or brief. We can expect, anticipate, and look forward to the low moments in our life, which will surely come, and we can be grateful for those tests in life that give us the opportunity to see what we're made of. But we must get rid of our false expectations that nothing bad will happen if we are to stay present and rise to those challenges.

When we are free from our own mind, everything we see becomes positive because we see it as a vehicle for further liberation. Dark and uncertain times become new territory to explore and discover. We can even be grateful for them.

We simply have to get out of that preconceived notion of how things should and shouldn't be.

The word "should" is maybe the number one word in our mind that leads to suffering more than any other because it says what reality should and shouldn't be.

It makes our little ideas about life bigger and wiser than the universe's. It traps us in dualistic thinking, either pitting us against the universe, or for it, depending on the moment. It leads to our attachment to whatever is pleasurable, and hatred for whatever is unpleasurable.

In reality, reality just is. And whatever it is, is perfect. It shouldn't be any other way because it is only this way. This is the only way it could have been and it couldn't have been any other way.

Every choice we make is based on our entire life experience before it. For one thing to change, it would all have to change, and we'd be living in a completely different universe, one where the laws of physics are not stable enough to evolve life. Rather, the universe would be unbalanced, and the laws that govern it would be unstable and bendable to one person's will — yours.

Instead, we live in a universe in which we cannot change reality. So, we have a choice. We either accept reality, deny it, or wholeheartedly and enthusiastically embrace it.

If we want to get out of our mental prison, we have to drop the "shoulds," and embrace whatever comes — fully, wholly and consciously — simply allowing whatever is, to be. And then we can respond with our intention, intuition, presence, wisdom, and with full and open hearts.

To deny reality is a form of insanity. And to wish it were some other way is like living in a fantasy world. This reality is so beautiful and is already perfect, even if we can't always see it. If we try to escape it (through things like entertainment, work, substances, etc...), we are only going to create dependence, depression, anxiety and stress because we cannot escape life.

The only reason we think life is not perfect is because we're living in the world of "shoulds" and "shouldn'ts." So it's important to recognize when our mind says things like, "This person shouldn't have done that thing," or "This country shouldn't be like this," or "my life should be different than this."

Every single inch of nature, the ocean, and the sky is beyond breathtakingly mesmerizingly beautiful, inspiring and uplifting. Everywhere humans didn't touch, the universe made it spectacular for us. This is proof we live in a loving and perfect universe. We have to embrace reality in order to see it. **The more we deny, try to escape, and resist life, the more we lose sight of its perfection.**

When we accept what is, embrace it, and even learn to love it, then we can actively engage and interact with this world as it is. Then we can work wiser and be more effective, because we're dealing with reality, not a fantasy. There's no stress because we're not resisting anything, and we can do it with peacefulness, love and joy within us. This is how we achieve our dreams, and bring about a more peaceful and loving world.

Life Lesson 17

You Are Not Your Trauma

You are not your trauma. You are not your circumstances. You are that eternal unchanging light of consciousness. Your true nature cannot be hurt. Your body can be hurt, your property can be lost, but nothing can touch the true you.

No matter what happens to you, no matter how terrible, there can be peace. There may be trauma, there may be hurt. But those are the mere shallow surfaces of your infinite vastness.

Sometimes when bad things happen to us, we feel like we deserved it or we brought it on ourselves. Some people think that it's their karma. The truth is, we live in a world that is slowly but surely raising its consciousness. A lot of people ask, "Why do bad things happen to me?" Or, "Why do bad things happen to good people?" And the truth is, we live in a quantum universe.

And as in quantum mechanics, our life unfolds as a wave of probability. If we eat healthfully, our probability of getting sick is much diminished, but not impossible.

Unfortunately, when we live in a world with some cruelty, sometimes cruelty happens to us. We didn't deserve it, we didn't ask for it, nobody deserves it, but it also makes us who we are today.

Many who have experienced profound trauma in their life subconsciously feel they have to carry their burden and pain with them forever so they can feel protected and safe. If they're always on guard, always vigilant, maybe they can prevent the trauma from happening again — this is the classic trauma response.

We think if we always keep it in the back of our mind, that we will be safe, but it actually makes everything in the world seem cruel, dangerous and unkind because we're always suspicious. This is why veterans can't leave their hypervigilance on the battlefield.

But I assure you that you can let that trauma go. You can leave it in the past. You can put that weight of the past down and still protect yourself.

Without the weight, you will still have the lessons you learned from it, but you don't have to relive it. You don't have to carry it.

Practice observing your thoughts and observing how your

mind brings you back there. Then, gently bringing your awareness back to the present moment can help you leave the past in the past.

It's so important to understand the nature of the mind by watching, without judgment, the patterns of our thoughts, and the nature of the mind and how it works. This creates understanding and an awareness into what is going on within us, it brings consciousness to our unconscious responses, and we can dive deeper into understanding who we are, why we are, and how to change.

Therapy and psychology can be immensely beneficial and essential for many people, but they cannot peer as deep into our psyche, or as clearly, as we can when we spend some time noticing the nature of our thoughts and mind. Only we have direct, unfiltered access to the most inner workings of our mind.

For most people, 99% of our lives are spent focusing on something outside of the mind. When we shine our light of awareness on itself; our unconscious, habitual, conditioned thinking ceases to exist. By simply becoming aware of thought patterns, we change them.

A very funny improv teacher once said to my class while we were working on creating original characters, **"Knowing how you are is knowing who you are."**

I don't know if he knew what a spiritual genius he was, but that was a very profound statement that can be applied way beyond an improv comedy class.

He was teaching us how to develop rich, three-dimensional characters off the cuff, but what he really taught me is that who we are is how we respond to what life throws our way. It's not the name, birthplace, religion, race or occupation that makes us who we are. It's how we respond to being all those things in the world we find ourselves in.

Our mind is like a wild animal, jumping from thought to thought, wildly and uncontrollably. If we are to catch our wild mind so that it can become calm, like casting a net over a wild animal, we have to know how the mind works. We have to study it, we have to anticipate it, and we have to stay present and alert. By understanding the mind's chaotic and impulsive ways, we can overcome those tendencies. By seeing how it gets lost in thought, we can prevent downward spirals. We can consciously choose to focus on what we want to focus on. We don't have to relive our darkest days over and over again. We can master our mind. And it starts by paying attention and being ready with that net.

You Are This Moment

Who are we? What are we? Where do we reside in this body? Why are we here and why is there suffering? What is this invisible pressure on our shoulders and how can we set it down?

Are we our name? People change their names.

Are we the roles we take on? Father, mother, husband, wife, son, daughter, brother, sister, etc...? Our roles constantly change as well, often many times a day.

Are we the collection of cells that make up our physical body? Every few years, all of our cells will change and become new cells.

Are we our memories? Memories fade and disappear.

Are we our preferences — our likes and dislikes? These change constantly, and what we liked as children we often

209

have no interest in today.

Are we our past or our future? We've never been in the past or the future. We've always only ever been in the present moment. Which only leaves one possibility.

We are this moment, fully and completely.

You may carry the weight of the world on your shoulders. You may have one foot in the past and one foot in the future. But the more you fully embrace this moment, the more you fully become present in the here and now.

This is how we fully become our true self, free from stress and worry, and free from the fictional concepts we place on ourselves, free from indecision and insecurity. We're no longer torn away from this moment and this place. We realize this is exactly where we're supposed to be, and everything is perfect the way it is.

The real you has no flaws or defects.

There is nothing you need to learn, acquire or achieve. You are already complete and whole.

A wise Zen Budhhist monk, Shunryu Suzuki, once said, "Each of you is perfect the way you are... and you can use a little improvement."

When we identify with the brain — our thinking mind — we're never enough. We're never smart enough or good enough. But when we realize that we are this moment, when we identify with the consciousness within us, all is understood.

True understanding is understanding that we don't need to understand.

On a thinking level, we don't understand how our bodies work. But when we are present in the moment, we can tap into the wisdom of billions of years of evolution. We instinctively know what to give our body.

We realize there is a higher wisdom at play than our thoughts. We see that we don't have to tell our blood to bring oxygen to every part of our body. We don't have to remember to tell our hearts to beat, our lungs to breathe, or our organs to function. It all knows.

This great wisdom is within us, effortlessly keeping these miraculous bodies alive and functioning.

When we're lost in thought, we make mistakes and bad choices. And we don't follow our heart, our instincts, or our inner compass, which knows more than the mind could ever comprehend. This is the wisdom of our DNA.

This wisdom of understanding arises in between thoughts and words, in the quiet stillness, and in the empty space between objects. It's in the underlying stillness and peace of the universe that makes all life possible.

We can experience this vast ocean of peace when we look up into the sky towards infinity, or when we close our eyes and turn our attention inwards. That same infinite depth is within us.

And who we are, that infinitesimally small point of consciousness shining outward and perceiving everything we experience, resides within you. It's the non-material, non-physical blank canvas of awareness from which all our senses are perceived. And only in this moment can we become aware of awareness itself.

Because time is merely an illusion created by our memory which records the past, and our imagination which anticipates the future, but those memories and fantasies are still only ever recalled in the present moment.

Every memory of the past and imagined future are but tiny fractions compared to the vastness of this moment where all of life's depth and richness lie. It's the difference between looking at a sketch on a sheet of paper, and going on a fully immersive thrill ride at Disney World.

Every breath we take is a doorway into this moment, and into ourselves.

Because every breath happens in the present moment, it transports us out of our past, out of the stories we tell about ourselves and about our lives; and it brings us into this moment, into who we really are — perfect miracles of life with infinite potential, infinite wisdom and understanding, beyond words, beyond labels, and beyond constructed identities to a place where our true nature of peace and love are revealed.

Healing From Trauma

Trauma is something we have all faced to some degree in our lives. You don't have to have been in war or physically hurt either. Whether it's a mean kid in school, an unfair teacher, parents divorcing, avoidance and neglect, or even changing cities as a child — all of these experiences have the potential to negatively shape how we see the world and stay with us for the rest of our lives.

So how can we get to the root of our trauma? How can we heal and move on? How can we stop the automatic stress response that occurs when our past trauma is triggered?

Today, there are many ways to heal from PTSD and trauma in our lives. Many people have found therapy, plant medicines, pharmaceuticals, and MDMA-assisted therapy to be extremely beneficial. All of these tools can be indispensable to finding lasting peace, especially when we find ourselves truly unable to help ourselves.

But for all of these treatments that rely on the external help of others or medicine, they do have a few drawbacks. They can be expensive, unavailable in certain areas, they can become dependencies, and we may be preventing ourselves from becoming our strongest, healthiest and happiest selves if we don't take the personal responsibility and find our own inner power within. If we use these treatments to avoid getting to the root, to avoid meditating on the nature of our trauma, then we actually delay our healing.

Something that is available to all of us right this very minute is meditation, introspection and self-reflection. This is how we discover our true infinite power to consciously create any change within us that we wish. Unlike medicine, there's no come down. These changes are permanent. Unlike the coping mechanisms we may learn from talking to a specialist (which again, can be wonderful and practical tools in their own right), when we rip out the roots through deep introspection, there's no growing back.

The spiritual method of healing is the one method that also makes us happier, calmer, kinder in our relationships, more focused at work, more creative and joyful, and more present for our brief and precious life — naturally, freely and permanently.

We can't fix a car if we don't look under the hood.

Yes, we can take our car to a mechanic, but if it breaks down in the middle of nowhere, we're in real trouble. Still though, it's just a car, which is why I always take mine to a mechanic for something as little as an oil change, but our bodies and brains are a bit more important.

Here's the good news. When we get to the root of a problem, it doesn't manifest in other ways in our lives. When we try to mask our symptoms by putting a bandaid over the problem, the roots often grow into other forms. Trauma can turn into addiction, rage, physical illness, impulsivity, and any disorder on the spectrum of mental health.

When we get to the real root of our suffering, all suffering stops. So we only have to do one thing to fix all our problems in life.

To do this, we have to look at the deepest parts of mind. We must become deeply conscious of our ego, our thoughts and emotions, and our triggers. We have to unload our mental gun so that a trigger has no power over us anymore.

We have to realize that triggers are our friend, showing us what we need to work on and what we're still holding onto. Unloading the gun means consciously creating a new response. With visualization, we can prepare ourselves for situations that would normally trigger a trauma response in us.

The more time we spend in meditation visualizing our difficult past, visualizing scenarios that trigger us, and visualizing how we wish to respond in the future, the easier it gets to avoid a trauma response.

Try to see every detail: the smells, the sounds, and how it feels. This creates muscle memory so it becomes automatic because to the brain, there is no difference between doing and imagining. According to multiple studies, doing nothing more than visualizing ourselves lifting weights can increase our muscle size and strength.

Visualization is how athletes prepare for games so they can react faster and in the most optimal way without even having to think about it. It is also a powerful tool for changing how we react to triggers.

The second thing we can do during our meditation is called analytical meditation, where we consciously explore the stories we relive over and over. This is how we become mindful of our thought processes.

We gain wisdom and insight into how we think, how we are behaving, and how the trauma feels in our body. We must observe the mental story, recognize what is not serving us, and let it go. We can change the story, accept it, and allow it so that we can heal from it.

No one has direct access to your mind except for you. The only problem is, we're mostly unaware of what's going on inside us. Once we become aware, we can become our own greatest, 24/7 therapist.

Honestly look at how you speak to yourself about your trauma. Do you identify with it as part of who you are? We tend to unconsciously think that identifying with our trauma will protect us from future trauma. But this only ends up keeping us traumatized.

The more we look at our trauma in the peaceful setting of our meditation, the more clearly we're able to see it, process it, and make peace with it.

This is not the quick fix, but it is the real fix. Be patient, allow memories to come up, and witness how the stress response diminishes over time. A combination of therapies may be right for you as well. There is no one way. What works for some does not work for others. We have to listen to our intuition — nobody is a bigger you expert than you.

Allow some space in your day for your mind to settle and reach a relaxed, meditative state. It's not quite asleep, not quite awake, but it allows our conscious mind to communicate with our subconscious and create lasting changes in how we respond to situations.

This is how we form new neural pathways in our brain that create new responses to triggering situations. The more we slow down — mentally and physically — the calmer and more peaceful our lives effortlessly become. This is the foundation for all healing.

We can even **use mantras which we repeat over and over again in our mind, such as, "I am safe, I am loved."**

Repetition, whether it's a mantra or a visualization, taps into our subconscious mind and is another way we can create permanent changes. Books like this one are great (if I may say so myself), but if we don't integrate it into a daily practice, we'll eventually forget what we read. So practice is key.

Most importantly, **when we observe our thoughts, think like a detective.** The thoughts we're aware of came from somewhere in our subconscious and unconscious mind.

All thinking stems from our conditioned past. So ask yourself, what in your subconscious could have made a certain thought arise into consciousness? What past experience is being brought up in the present moment unconsciously?

We can dissect what is going on under the surface through these clues, through the emotions we feel, and the thoughts we think. The more we study our own mind — like anything else we study — the more we learn and grow in wisdom. So spend some time focusing on your mind — that place where all of the trauma is coming from — and then we can truly start to heal.

Life Lesson 18

You Can't Possess Life, You Are Life

Our physical bodies, our minds and thoughts, and this physical universe all fall prey to the laws of karma — cause and effect. What preceded this moment led to this moment. But space, silence, and our pure conscious awareness are eternal and unchanging. This is the nature of our true selves. When we realize this, we become truly free.

We are the life that animates these bodies. It's not "my" life or "your" life. You can't possess something you are. You can't have a relationship with yourself, only with something that exists outside of yourself. We simply are life.

Like a tree knows how to grow and thrive, all the knowledge and wisdom we need is already inside each and every one of us. You don't have to read any books or belong to any religion. This wisdom is universal and available to every one of us.

Relationships involve an object and a subject. Whenever we say things like, "my body," "my brain," my mind," or "my thoughts," we know for a fact that we must be talking about something that is not truly who we are.

It is an illusion because our real self is formless. The word "my" implies an owner and an object. So we cannot be these things.

We just are. We are love, we are life, without any relationship at all to love or life because we are love and life.

That means we can never lose our life or love either. They will be us for as long as there is an us. So whenever we are loving ourselves or hating ourselves, we are forgetting our true selves.

Human beings live mostly in the egoic mind, identifying with our thinking brain rather than our awareness, which creates a duality, almost like a split personality, because now there is us and our ego. Schizophrenic thoughts become common, such as, "I'm so upset with myself," or, "I'm incredibly happy with myself," which is the clearest indication that we've created a separateness, a division within our own psyche that says me and my ego are separate.

As we identify more with awareness, we develop a deeper understanding about ourselves and the true nature of others as well, and understanding is the foundation that love is built upon. The ego on the other hand is frequently our own worst critic, treating ourselves in ways we would never let anyone else treat us, and saying things about ourselves we would never let anyone else say about us.

As we identify with our true selves, all divisions disappear. Instead of being a person of a particular race, gender, religion, age, height, attractiveness, economic class, etc..., you just are. You're not a temporary physical form. You're an eternal being of consciousness — the miracle of life.

So, instead of identifying as a physical form which comes with labels and judgments, instead of having this duality and division, we can feel a sense of wholeness and oneness. We can see that we're all one universal consciousness shining through a temporary physical body.

Understanding Who We Are

If you are not your thoughts, and if you are not your body, who are you? Where is the "you" within you?

Every single thing about us undergoes constant change from moment to moment, and yet something remains steady through the change. That light of consciousness, that animating life force, never changes, never flickers, and never dims our entire life. This is the eternal you. When the body dies and dissolves, that energy still exists, like how electricity never ceases to exist. It never disappears.

Most of us identify with our thoughts. We believe we are our mind and we believe we must be inside our head somewhere, but this is an illusion simply caused by our eyes being in our head. We know that our mind mostly thinks unconsciously, unintentionally and automatically. Sometimes it thinks totally crazy things we would never say or do. We could be waiting for the subway and a thought pops into our mind, "I could push this guy into the subway and murder him and no one would even know." We would never really murder that person. But the mind, without awareness, is an unconscious, wild, thinking machine.

When we think with intention and consciousness, like when we tell ourselves positive and beneficial things such as, "I did a great job at that meeting," this reveals who we are far more than unconscious thoughts.

When we put our intention and conscious awareness onto our thinking, then our true self is revealed because we are being mindful and present, using all of our faculties, intuition and instinct, and not just mindlessly thinking.

When we're not conscious and present, we accidentally hurt people, we speak unkindly, and we are a slave to the mind's impulses and habits.

We can't truly hear, see, or think because we are listening to the world's most repetitive, negative, and pointless audiobook in our head, and we are totally absorbed and lost in it.

This is what it means to be spiritually asleep, unconscious, lost in a dream inside our own mind instead of experiencing real life. Any label, judgment, thought or opinion removes us from reality.

To awaken is to actually shut off the mind. This is how we begin to identify as the animating lifeforce energy that inhabits these bodies. Of course we are that electric energy that turns these bodies on, because when we die, that is what disappears — everything that made us who we are. The body and brain, without that energy/spirit/consciousness, is nothing more than worm food. That invisible nonmaterial presence is everything.

Without consciousness, we would be robots. We would be like a video camera recording footage but no one's there to look at it, so the footage is never seen and really doesn't exist. It falls into the void of nothingness.

But because we have something that no machine yet has, consciousness, we have a sense of self — someone's at home inside watching the show. That is the true nature of who we are.

Consciousness, that light bulb in the film projector that shines its light through the film reel to make the movie appear on the screen, creates the illusion of movie magic. When that bulb goes out, the movie goes off. The film still exists, but there's no way to perceive it. We are that light of consciousness — the same light that's in you, me and everyone else — creating the entire universe around us.

Scientists have been looking for centuries to find out where consciousness comes from. We know which part of the brain can convert light into electrical signals in the brain that represent a visual image. We know how the brain can convert sound waves from the eardrum into electrical brain signals.

But we don't know where in the brain or body those signals turn into the qualities of the images we see, or the music and words we experience hearing.

No scientist has been able to find it because the truth is, it doesn't exist in the material sense. It arises from our life force energy — our light of awareness.

We are the creators and receivers all at once; the universal consciousness and the finite point of awareness. We are the narrator, writer, director and lead actor in our story; while simultaneously working for the big studio head (God/universe), who is also us.

So when we sit in meditation, and we practice not doing, just being and perceiving, this puts us in touch with the true nature of who we are. This helps us know ourselves.

And it helps us to identify more with the perceiver, observer, witness of our lives — our true self — rather than identifying with what we are witnessing — these bodies, these thoughts, and our experiences.

We can see our bodies, hear our thoughts, but who we are is the higher intelligence, that higher consciousness which arises when we're present and out of our head, not absorbed in our thoughts. The brain is always grasping for answers, taking sides, all to strengthen the ego. But true understanding is understanding there's no need to understand.

We think thinking will lead to understanding, but thinking only leads to more confusion and inner unrest. In present moment awareness, we see all, know all, and it is always peaceful. This is how we relax into clarity, when all the answers can be revealed. When we practice living in this state of alert observation without mental reaction, inner peace is inevitable. It doesn't mean we stop thoughts, it means we stop unconscious, unmindful, unproductive, chaotic and stressful thoughts.

As we spend more and more time as the witness, we begin to notice if we're being our biggest fans, or our biggest haters. Are we rooting for ourself, or sabotaging ourself? With awareness, we can love the film even when it's a little slow and boring, trust the film even through dark moments, and know that the big studio head in the sky wants us all to enjoy the show.

We think that the world we see is being projected onto our mind. But the truth is, our mind is projected onto the world.

Everything we see and experience is a projection of our mind.

Our experiences are always seen through the lens of our past, our conditioning, our trauma, and the story about our life that we tell ourselves. Simply becoming aware of this fact helps us recognize our place within our experience, it lessens our identification with the "I" of the ego, and we become aware of the infinite power of our awareness. With presence, and with the help of meditation and mindful living, we can see through the clouds of thoughts that obscure our view, and we can observe life as the miracle it truly is.

Life Lesson 19

Every Moment Is a Miracle

The way of wise living is to never forget that every moment is a miracle. That is the goal of spirituality, to never forget.

Mental health is about how we process our experiences. But spirituality is the quality of experience itself.

With mental health, we can function and get through the day. It helps us blow off steam in a healthy way, and that is vital for dealing with life's challenges.

But with spirituality comes love and joy. It changes how

we see the world so that challenges become welcomed friends, not enemies that stress us out. It's great to destress, but it's even better to not take on new stress in the first place.

By seeing the world as beautiful and magical and special and sacred and precious, our mental health can even improve because spirituality goes to the very root of our experience.

It is consciousness taking a look at itself, turning inwards, and staying in touch with the deeper peace beneath whatever chaos we're witnessing.

When we do this, we realize how insignificant our stressful meeting at work was. Or that mean thing that the driver yelled at us on the road. We can become deeply familiar with this calm, changeless, eternal light within us, this higher consciousness and expanded awareness that goes beyond the illusory physical world and into the spiritual.

It is always in the stillness where we find peace and strength. The mind is like an ocean, and beneath the crashing violent waves on the surface is a deep, calm, silent ocean, infinitely deep.

Mental health tries to calm the storm, and thank goodness it does, but the spiritual dimension within us goes much deeper.

It is in this deeply calm state with no thoughts, only a pure focus on the present moment, and tapped into that eternal light within, that time stops. When we no longer compare this moment to the last, when we no longer wish for the future to arrive, we experience eternity in an instant. Boredom and agitation disappear as infinite patience and peace fill us.

When we get out of our heads and tap into our deepest

understanding and wisdom, we can hear the whispers of our intuition in our heart and awaken to the instincts coming from our gut.

Every culture throughout history that was in tune with their bodies understood the intelligence of our intuitive hearts and our gut feelings. Oftentimes, these cultures respected our brain's confused thinking the least. Today, we are a head first culture.

When we experience the void — that deep ocean of peace we enter in deep meditation or in moments of pure awareness and presence — nothing exists to us except that peaceful inner space.

If you were floating in deep space and there was nothing else around as far as you could see, you wouldn't know if you were upside down or sideways.

You wouldn't be able to comprehend the passage of time because time is measured by the Earth rotating and revolving around the sun.

We can only understand time and our place in the universe through our relation to something else. In our normal thinking mind, as thoughts chatter on constantly, we have a sense of time passing because we can measure it by our thinking. When a sentence is thought, we understand a few seconds have passed. When we've really been overthinking, paragraph after paragraph, it can feel like minutes or hours. But in pure stillness, there is no time, there is no physical dimension. There is only you, the eternal, infinite and formless.

For me, spirituality has helped me see that the only constant is change, that there is only transformation in this physical universe. There is no beginning and no end. There is nothing to be attached to because everything is impermanent, and nothing to resist because it's all temporary anyway.

When we can experience our deepest bliss, pure joy and love, without the thinking mind coming in trying to label it and disrupting that peace, time stops, problems stop, and fear stops.

Eternal, infinite beings do not have fear, insecurity, stress, doubts or anger. They don't need substances or escapism for their joy. They don't need to unload their problems because they don't have any and everything they need, they know they have within.

It doesn't matter if we live for one second or 100 more years because in that timeless dimension there is only pure love.

All that matters is how present we were, how much of that love we felt, and how much we enjoyed each moment (here, "enjoy" doesn't mean living like there's no tomorrow. It means living fully while tending to our lives with wisdom and peace).

Meditation helps us discover that stillness so we can turn into a constant state of being. We become grateful for each moment, and through repeated practice it rewires our brain to be more present and peaceful as our natural way of life.

When we live in time, we are finite bodies. When we become still, we become limitless. With stillness, we can rise to any occasion with calm and confidence. We never act out, we're never impulsive, and we never lose ourselves to heavy emotions. This timeless way of being, and flowing with the present moment instead of grasping at time, is the only way we can have direct experience of life and this universe.

If we look closely at one minute, we see that it can be divided into infinite moments. 1 second can be divided in two, and then again, and again, and again forever. The closer we look for a single moment, the more we realize that it doesn't exist, because time doesn't exist. There is just eternal presence.

If there are infinite moments in one minute, then there is eternity in every moment

This gives rise to an appreciation for every breath, every moment, and every experience; instead of fear or worries about that ticking clock towards our inevitable demise.

Not only is each moment infinitely divisible, but each moment also has a beginning, a middle and an end — that's three more divisions for every infinite moment. The closer we look, the clearer it becomes that there is no time, only the one eternal stream of presence. Only our brain's imagination of a future and memory of the past create the illusion of time. Everything is always now, as embers or seeds, forever existing as the endless cycle of change.

So this notion of dying only matters if we haven't touched that timeless, formless dimension within us. When we recognize the eternal nature of life going on and simply changing forms, then there's nothing to be afraid of. That's the beauty that spirituality shows us.

Even one moment of presence and peace is priceless.

Many of us, especially toward the end of our lives, would love to have had a few more moments of peace, chances to be present a bit more with our family, and so on. But this stems from a fear and misunderstanding about our final destination. Peace is found by focusing on the journey, the here and now, and then almost magically, those moments we do have will become more peaceful, longer, and more frequent. This is how we see eternity in each moment.

When we are in total bliss, there is no room for craving for more bliss or longer bliss. We're too happy to think about any of that stuff. **So by letting go of any desired outcome, suddenly the desired outcome appears out of nowhere.**

Everything you need to know and do will be clear in the moment if you are fully present, out of your head, and with enough mental space to receive the answer.

So letting go becomes the simplest and most profound way to clear space. Whatever you are observing, observe it with deep curiosity. In this way, you are not thinking, you are in the present moment.

Becoming Aware of Awareness

Awareness is like a muscle. It takes practice and training to learn to truly observe, which requires being truly present. The second we make commentary in our mind, we stop observing and we start clouding our observation with these thought constructs.

The more we meditate. The more aware we become. The more we observe our breath, the more subtleties we discover and the more heightened our senses become.

We learn that no two breaths are the same, and we become more attuned to our body.

This expanded awareness, where we become highly aware of nuances and details, is the end of boredom. Even if we're looking at a blank wall, we'll see there's still so much to observe and appreciate: the texture, the light and atmosphere, our own thoughts and feelings that it causes to arise.

There is infinite uniqueness in each moment, endless ways to look at a blank wall. We can look from a distance and admire the building materials and craftsmanship, or close up and appreciate the details.

It can be either a beautiful blank canvas for us to project our loving imagination, or a boring stressful wall of empty loneliness. We get to choose. We get to create our reality, and that is the beauty of life.

The more aware we become of subtleties, the more we notice all the little sounds and smells, and the richer our life becomes. With heightened awareness, colors become more vibrant and everything comes alive.

We start to notice the relationships and connections between people and objects. We expand our consciousness to see the impact our actions will have, not just narrowly seeing the actions without understanding their consequences. By doing so, we can always make the best choices in each moment in order to create the world around us that we want to live in.

Awareness is about being aware of the infinite by simultaneously being aware of the present — our mind, body and surroundings.

We can be aware of all the activities taking place on earth, everything that ever happened and everything that will happen. We no longer see a cup, we see the miners, the manufacturing plant, the cargo shippers, and the whole global economy. We see what will happen to the cup after ten years, a hundred, and a thousand.

In this state of pure and total awareness, there is zero

room in the mind for thoughts, negativity, anxiety, depression, worry or doubt. We become beings of infinite understanding.

Every Moment is a Miracle and So Are You

Reality is no more than a wave of energy interpreted by the brain to create a simulated universe in our mind. Our brains are the receivers, converting "cosmic WiFi" into electrical signals projected to our consciousness. You are not a physical being, you are the light of awareness — a point of attention in the infinite sea of consciousness, temporarily experiencing the simulated universe as an illusory body.

We don't see the truth. We don't see reality. These physical bodies were designed to see food, danger, and potential mates. That is why we are able to live and survive. But never forget your limitlessness and that you create your reality. There is only oneness in the great expanse of consciousness. There is no solidity, time, space, distance or existence without a brain to construct it. The universe is a wave of infinite probability. What will you create from it?

Your thoughts are hallucinations, a spontaneous voice projected into your mind that is not real. We think insanity is seeing people that aren't there, or hearing voices. But we all hear a voice in our head that convinces us that it is us, and we all believe it even though it often says things we know are crazy, it subverts our true intentions, and it manipulatively tries to control us,

This is a form of modern mass insanity. **Only by learning to quiet and tame the mind can we evolve.** When you learn to welcome every challenge and difficulty as an opportunity to grow and learn, no hardship or pain can generate suffering.

Stress is very stressful. When we get stressed, we desperately want it to stop right away! But when we accept that life will be at times stressful and unhappy, we can playfully explore our stress and unhappiness with curiosity and peace. Then, immediately and magically, we're no longer stressed. **Stress only hangs around where it's not wanted.**

The way you see the world is a projection of your mind and what is inside you. If you see beauty and kindness, it's because you have touched the beauty and kindness within you. All you have to do is close your eyes to disconnect from the material world and enter this spiritual place — our home — loving and peaceful everywhere we go.

Everything, the entire universe, is within each of us. So dive in and go find that love and kindness. Be the love you wish to receive, and receive it you shall. Remember your power, that you are always in control of your focus. And never forget that you are a miracle.

Life Lesson 20

Death Is the Last Adventure

Death is the beginning of the last great adventure and exploration of humanity. Every person gets to explore this thing that no living person knows about. Death in itself is a beautiful process. It's like being born.

Death is the great equalizer. No matter how rich or how poor, we're all going in the same direction, to the same place.

There are many different religions, each with different ideas about what comes next. As humans, we naturally feel comforted by the idea that bad people will be punished and good people will be rewarded. When we look around, past people's wealth and their longevity, we can see that people do reap what they sow.

This doesn't mean that a peaceful person will be able to avoid conflict or pain, but it does mean that they will be able to make peace with whatever circumstances they find themselves in.

A person who only cares about money and power will surely live a loveless and joyless life, because they nurtured their greed and lust instead.

They may be praised and feared by their family, but that will not comfort an angry person who only knows selfishness. They may enjoy an assortment of high quality drugs and sexual partners, but that will not give them lasting fulfillment. It's often the people who look like they have it all are the ones who are the most depressed.

Once we let go of our false idea of a "good" life, we can clearly see karma play out in this one single lifetime. No one escapes their own heart.

Just as we see patterns in nature repeating in endless microcosms of each other, like how one thing dying gives rise to so much more life, and how time has no beginning or end, we can also sense from these repeating patterns that when our consciousness is no longer confined to a separate body, it merges back into the one universal consciousness of infinite wisdom and knowledge.

The punishment for living a cruel life may be nothing more than the eternal awareness and shame of our own cruelty. **We are not responsible for what we are not aware of, but eventually all will become known.**

We know that individual parts (us) can never be separated from the whole (oneness), like how all the parts of an engine are needed for the car to run. So too, we are never truly separate, and the cycle from oneness to separateness goes on forever.

No one can avoid the consequences of their actions. This is made plainly clear in our universe. That's not to say that bad things won't happen to good people or that good things won't happen to bad people — it happens everyday.

There's no avoiding pain in this life for anyone. How we respond — internally and externally — determines the quality of our life, not the stuff that happens.

Life is everything to everyone, and we decide what matters and what's important. This is the beauty of life. It's ours to make as we wish. This is the freedom we all have but that the materialistic media tells us we don't have.

And we can see death as either the terrifying unknown, or a wonderful part of life that makes everything possible.

Death makes way for the newer generation, which is generally more enlightened than the last. Pain tells us what to avoid and joy tells us what to seek.

So all of it, life and death, it's all a beautiful process. Everything in life is death and rebirth, and this is why we have constant change, why no bad situation lasts forever, and why life can continue to march on.

We are recyclers, converting the plants into energy, and turning that energy into soil for the future. **Death *is* life.** A tiger doesn't murder a gazelle. The gazelle gives life to the tiger, the insects, the vultures and the bacteria, all of which are integral parts of this delicate ecosystem. It is simply nature rolling onward.

Confronting death is one of the hardest parts of living. Grief and tragic loss can define the rest of our lives. But death itself is a beautiful process, as precious as being born.

Everybody lives on forever because life lives on forever, and we're all the same lifeforce energy, not just on this planet, but every planet with life, in every universe, and even after this universe collapses and re-expands, there we will be.

It's so common to fear the unknown and fear what we don't understand, but the unknown is the most important thing we can come to accept because it's the only truth there is. We are infinitely intuitive beings with very limited knowledge.

If we resist the unknown, if we fear what we don't understand, we fall prey to stories — positive or negative — whichever speaks to us based on our past experiences. But stories are information, pointers and signposts, never the truth. Truth comes from trust.

When you have full trust and faith in the universe, there's nothing to fear.

Death is something that, whether we like it or not, lives with us at all times in our lives. It's something that we're constantly aware of, even if we're not aware that we're aware of it. It drives our quest for food and resources, without which we would die. Death drives our ambitions and our labor, because that will earn us our resources to live.

But on a deeper level, it is not death that drives us, it is our misunderstanding of death. When we live our lives focused only on the physical material world, death looks scary, like we disappear into oblivion. When we notice the nature of all things, when we observe the nature of the universe at its deepest level, we can develop a deep understanding of the true nature of death as well. **The better we understand death, the more we can understand life.**

Understanding Death

All fear stems from the fear of death. Fear of not earning enough money is ultimately about survival and fear of death.

Fear of public speaking is the fear that our ego — who we think is us — will die if we make a bad speech. Fear of spiders is all about the fear of dying too.

But death, this thing we spend our whole lives trying not to think about, is not as scary as it seems. We're so afraid to even look at or think about death that we've imagined it to be far worse than it actually is.

The truth is, the only constant is change. There is only transformation. There is no beginning and no ending. These are facts.

Death has been the main driver of human behavior for millennia. It's why we survived as a species, why we stayed away from tigers, from the edge of cliffs, went foraging for food, worked so hard, got a good job, earned money, and built or bought a house. These are all drivers from our fear of death and not wanting to die. And so even a rational fear of death can be a wonderful thing.

Clearly it is an essential part of life that we will die. But simultaneously existing with that fear is an innate love for life that also drives everything we do.

It is the other side of the coin, inseparable from the other side. But we are not always mindful of that positive drive.

Unchecked, fear can consume us and lead to many phobias. It can lead us to not taking chances, and living a safe and small life. But however we live, we will all reach that final destination. There is no point in fearing the inevitable and we can make peace with death. Death is only scary if we fail to understand that it is an illusion based on our lack of knowledge.

We can either trust in the universe, trust that it doesn't make mistakes, that the process of death is as beautiful as being born, or we can, in ignorance, fear it, which means to fear living a full life as well.

Overcoming the Fear of Death

The fear of death is such a powerful force in our society. It motivates so much of our activities, from selfishness and greed to cruelty and cowardice. We feel like we should be afraid of death because of our inherent urge to live. But the truth is, fearing the inevitable is a form of insanity. It's like fearing getting older. But fear only ends up blocking us from being able to appreciate reality and life as it is.

The best way to overcome the fear of death is to think of it as an adventure and a journey, which it is. Every journey brings excitement and optimism exactly because of its unknowable nature. If we knew what we were going to experience, there'd be no point in going anywhere. If we're terrified, it will be bad before it starts. If we're open, we'll be able to face anything.

Buddhists utilize a few different techniques to overcome the fear of death. Through rigorously testing these methods and debating them, they have honed them to perfection over the millennia.

One method is a particular death meditation. They will visualize everyone they know and love and everyone on Earth dying, including themselves.

They will meditate on time passing and the impermanent nature of all things. This is how they make peace with something that is normally too scary to think about.

It's not enough to know intellectually that all things will cease to be, we must meditate on this fact until we know it in the deepest parts of ourself.

Another thing Buddhists do, which is a bit more extreme but equally powerful, is they will go to the morgue or the crematorium where there are a lot of dead people, and they will meditate among the dead bodies. This is also a way to make peace with the cyclical nature of life.

Something we can all do that is a bit more practical, is to meditate in nature and ponder the soil — the death which gives life to everything.

In the West, we do our best to hide death. We don't think about it. When someone dies, we cover them with a blanket. The coroner's office or the funeral home picks up the body. If it's an open casket funeral, they will put makeup on the body and dress it as if it's still alive. We spend very little time thinking of death or being surrounded by death.

In Mexico and South America, they actually celebrate the Day of the Dead where they honor their ancestors. But in the United States and much of the West, we have this hands off, don't look, don't think about it attitude that leads to a lot of our fear.

Anything we don't think about or have experience with, we have an ignorance of. The best thing we can do is cherish the life we have without attachment, and recognize death as the end of suffering and a beautiful part of life.

It makes as much sense to be afraid of death as it does to be afraid of the sunrise. It's coming, it's inevitable, it's normal, and it's nothing to fear.

Life Lesson 21

We Have All Been Everybody

We've all been everybody and we'll all be everybody.

When the Buddha attained enlightenment, he had a sudden recollection of his infinite past lives. He remembered living as a myriad of humans, animals, deities and other metaphysical beings. Once, when sitting to give spiritual teachings, the Buddha shared, "I practiced the Ten Perfections for countless aeons."

An aeon or eon is a timespan of significant length. Some understand it to be a billion years, others the lifetime of a universe, and others as metaphor for a very long time. When asked how long it was, the Buddha replied that an aeon is the length of time it would take a granite mountain seven miles high and seven miles wide to completely erode away by nothing more than a man wiping it with the most delicate silk cloth once every one hundred years.

In Hinduism, an aeon has been described as the amount of time it would take to fill an empty cube 16 miles wide with mustard seeds if one seed were placed in it every hundred years.

According to one mathematician, this would take 1.7 trillion years, far older than the age of this universe. But even according to that timespan, it is still a drop in the buck of eternity.

Because time has no beginning or ending, because space is infinite, and because the past and present and future are all one, the Buddha could sense this expansive nature of reality.

He felt the infinite manifestations of this one life. He deeply understood the cyclical unending birth and rebirth that all physical matter submits to — the law of constant change.

From priests to murderers, princes to paupers, critters to creatures, the Buddha sensed his infinite lives, his evolution, and his countless lifetimes that it took to reach the level of a Buddha, or an awakened one.

But these weren't just past lives. They were past, present and future, as he understood that they are all deeply interconnected and one. Time only appears linear to a human mind with memory and imagination. But there is only the eternal present, all at once forever.

The Buddha did not say he saw a billion past lives. He

said countless, infinite, all. To me, this leaves no room for debate: he was everybody, will be everybody, and we are that lifeforce that has multiplied into every lifeform that ever was and ever will be. I am the Buddha, you are the Buddha, but we also had to be Hitler so we could get to Buddha.

This isn't just the Buddha's realization that I am recalling. This is my own observation from a deep reflection into the nature of who we truly are. It is only our physical bodies and our experiences that make up the subtle differences between all living things.

At our core, we are life, one life, in an unbroken chain dating back to the first single-celled organism, birthed from stardust, which started as energy released from one point in space at the Big Bang.

Depending on our attachment to these physical bodies and to our own man-made identities, we can either tap into the awareness of the universal infinite consciousness, or we can be trapped in our limited separate finite consciousness. The Buddha had become completely free from any physical or circumstantial conditioning.

The Buddha realized what scientists are now beginning to understand — that the universe had no beginning, and it may have existed in states of expansion and contraction for eternity.

He understood the concepts of quantum entanglement — how everything is connected — before microscopes existed. And he understood what theoretical physicists are already predicting, which is that we live in an infinite multiverse.

Life never began, life will never end, and it is all one, like a net connecting everything. Each part affects the whole, and the whole affects every part. When we expand our conscious awareness to the whole, everything makes sense. When we only focus on our own little mesh, fear and anger and greed arise. As the whole, we are invincible.

The universe is an ocean of energy. We always mistake the waves as being somehow separate, but there is only oneness.

When we look deeply into what all matter is made of, we discover only energy — flowing energy — unbroken, connected, endless and formless, pervading everything. There is no stuff, there is no matter, there is no empty space, and there is nothing separate from everything.

The ocean is our greatest spiritual teacher. We are the waves, rising and returning, rising and returning, but always the ocean. It may be stormy on the surface, but there is always a much more vastly deep peace, silence and spaciousness beneath the tumultuous waves, and it is still part of us. **Never forget you are the ocean.**

Another way to think about this is to consider a river. A river is not a river. A river is the ocean that evaporated and became clouds. It is the sun that evaporated the ocean. It is the rain that poured down. It is the mountains that collected the rain, and the valleys that cradled the river. Everything is everything. Nothing is separate.

When we meditate on what it would be like to be our ancestors, we are sensing our past. When we meditate on the existence of a plant, we are witnessing our genetic memory, encoded in our DNA.

Everything that ever was exists in every moment and in every point of space. When we become fully present, we step outside of our thoughts and limited perspective and we can tap into that field of consciousness beyond us.

That ocean we live in is a sea of consciousness, proven by the double-slit experiment. This field of energy and intelligence that surrounds us and moves through us guides our thoughts and actions, whether we are aware of it or not.

Just as the ants and bees know exactly what to do without thinking, we do too. It is only the limitations of the thinking mind that confuses us.

All answers appear when the questions disappear, but we have to quiet our mind to hear them.

To be present is to be connected with the universe, and to be lost in our head is to disconnect. Every single problem we have, every difficulty, every negative emotion and bad habit stems from this illusion of separateness.

When we feel one with everyone and everything, greed stops, lust stops, anger and hatred stops, impulsive behavior and bad habits even stop because we no longer exist in a vacuum where we can harm ourselves and believe there will be no consequences.

This is no belief system you have to believe in. There is no leap of faith here. It is something knowable through deep introspection and observation, which are essential for critical thinking and scientific inquiry.

Just because fish cannot see the ocean doesn't mean that it's not there. We didn't know that such a thing as air existed for thousands or millions of years. Today, we know that everything is a continual flow of energy, and yet we still dismiss it as unimportant.

Have you ever wondered how it was that you grew up as you, in your unique circumstances, and how impossibly improbable it was that you would be you. Surely a prince has wondered how remarkably unlikely and fortunate it was to be born a prince. But for each of us, the odds are equally as improbable that we would grow up with our parents and in our location at this unique time in history.

When you realize we are everyone, have been everyone and will be everyone, then the odds are 100%. Instead of wondering how we could've been born in a certain place at a certain time to certain parents, we can see plainly that in this quantum world of probability, in this stage of evolution — both personal evolution and collective evolution — that we too submit to the laws of probability. Like a caterpillar turning into a butterfly, we too have a ladder to climb.

When we look with clarity, all becomes clear. We see that the purpose of life is not riches or pleasure. It is learning.

Everyone on earth is here to learn and grow. Like the caterpillar that must dissolve into goo so that it can become a butterfly, our challenges are what make our transformation possible.

Sometimes those challenges come from lesser evolved people. But when we see ourselves in them, compassion rises. When we see ourselves in our heroes, courage arises.

Look deeper to see the same humanity in everyone, past their trauma and neural pathways. Look even deeper to see the same life and consciousness in all animals and plants, all wanting to live, protect their families, and create a more beautiful world for the future. I know I would do what you've done if I had your body, brain and experiences. I know you would do precisely as I do with my brain, body and experiences.

So there is something deeper guiding each one of us. The question is whether we can become present and truly connect on a deep level, instead of reacting based on our past habitual thinking and only seeing the surface differences.

Electricity is all around us, concentrated and channeled into our electronics and bringing them to life. Lifeforce energy (consciousness) is all around us, concentrating within us and animating these electrical bodies we have. We didn't make the energy. It was around long before us and will be here long after. We are its manifestations. What we manifest is what it has manifested through us. We are so much larger than an individual, and we are quite literally everyone and everything.

Life Lesson 22

Stillness is Everything

Imagine a movie where the camera is shaking all the time. It would be the worst movie you've ever seen. You wouldn't be able to focus on anything that was going on and you'd probably walk out in five minutes.

Stillness is everything. It's an opportunity to observe our chaotic mind and allow it to settle down no matter what else is happening.

Stillness is what allows for peace and calm, not the content of our experience. With a small perspective and limited consciousness, we see everything as shaky and turbulent, like the stormy surface of the ocean, unaware of the quiet calm beneath the waves.

Zoomed in, life seems chaotic. We see the drama, the fights, the yelling, the car crashes, and so on. But from space, everything seems peaceful on Earth. From even farther, we're no more than a blue dot floating in blackness.

When a camera is zoomed in very close, the slightest bump renders becomes magnified and it looks like a 50 magnitude earthquake.

By zooming out, seeing the bigger picture, and gaining some perspective, we can maintain a still, peaceful state. All it takes is expanding our awareness to the causes that led to this moment, and the effects that this moment will later cause.

It's not living in the past or the future; it's seeing both in the now. It's about more deeply seeing the truth of this moment.

Stillness is essential to expanding our awareness. It's the only way we can see beyond what is within our eyesight. Not thinking gives rise to the awareness of our own awareness. In stillness, we can connect the dots between various concepts and a deeper understanding emerges. We become highly aware of both what we know, what we don't know, and the impact that our words and actions will have.

Our minds can only think one word at a time. This means in each moment, one word takes up our entire attention and frame of view.

This is a very myopic, zoomed in, limited perspective. Sometimes we do need to think deeply about a problem, but today we act as though there's always a problem needing to be solved. This is stressful! Uncontrolled, unconscious thinking is unproductive. Intentional, conscious thinking is essential for human survival.

We as a species must become intentional with our thinking if we are ever going to solve the problems that unconscious thinking has caused in this world.

Most of us live our whole life on the surface of the ocean, never peering into the depth. We tend to live completely focused on, and lost in, the material world.

Unless we carve out some time for stillness in our life — either through meditation, looking at the sky, spending time in the peaceful quiet of nature, or even doing our chores with full presence and attention — we won't even know that stillness exists.

All of our physical needs and desires can be filled on the surface world, but they cannot create lasting, permanent peace and happiness.

The material world will only lead us on an endless chase for pleasure — an unwinnable race on a hamster wheel. A burger or a chocolate cake doesn't taste good after you've eaten it.

But stillness, both internal and external, will actually make the chaos in our lives feel more peaceful, and will lead to a richer and deeper dimension to our life.

To invite peace into our lives, we start with turning our attention to the nonmaterial: stillness, empty space (both within us and outside of us), and silence.

Silence is a gift that has become all too rare in our loud mechanical society. It's our beautiful doorway to peace. It allows us to become aware of the chaotic mind and gives it a chance to settle. Silence connects us to the peace of the universe.

Inner silence is our natural state when we are free from any agitation. Today, most of us live in constant agitation, but this is not our destiny.

When we explore the nonmaterial, we discover a deep peace that is always available to us. This spiritual dimension is not equally as important as all the stuff we know and love. It's more important. It's the space that allows all forms to emerge.

The silence allows us to perceive all the sounds that we hear. If there were no silence, we would be overwhelmed with sound at all times, and we wouldn't be able to make out any words or sounds. If there was no space, there would be no room for anything to exist.

It is space, stillness, and silence which create the room for all physical phenomena to emerge.

Most of us have no awareness of the deep peace and stillness that lies beneath all the chaos. We spend very little time aware of the connections and relationships between physical phenomena, and it's the relationships that determine how we experience the world. In wise relation to the world around us, we live rightly. In poor relation, we live in a hell of our own making.

It's no wonder we don't have peace on Earth. Most people actually can't stand peace. As soon as there is a moment of silence, our minds get racing trying to fill it up with something. We immediately pull out our phones, stir up some drama, or go figure out something to do to fill up the space or else we'll freak out and lose our minds.

Most people find peace very upsetting, disturbing, and discomforting. How long can most people enjoy silence and stillness? A minute at most? This is the state of the world and we see it reflected in our global conflicts, national conflicts, and communal and family conflicts.

We must stop being strangers to silence and enemies to peace if this planet is going to survive. We must make peace with peace.

When we are in a quiet space and our eyes are closed, we can touch the infinite space that exists within us. Just like how we make friends with new people, the more time we spend in this space, the more familiar it becomes and the more connected to it we become. This is our true nature, and the harder it is to sit in stillness, the more we need to practice and get back to ourselves.

We're not the body and thoughts we observe; we are the light of consciousness that sees.

Consciousness is the non-physical, energy, light of consciousness that resides in our body and gives life to our body. You are not the body that sees, you are the consciousness which perceives sight. Your true self perceives what your body senses. Everything physical changes constantly, but consciousness is the unchanging constant throughout your life. Consciousness is the stillness from which our physical world can be perceived.

Our bodies are like computers, but consciousness is the operator. When we are in autopilot mode, when the computer is running itself, we succumb to habitual behaviors. When we shine our consciousness onto what we're doing, we take back the reins. Becoming present is no different than developing a new habit, a new way of being. All it takes is intention plus practice.

Consciousness has baffled scientists for millennia. There's a saying that the more books there are written about something, the less we understand it. No one is writing books today on gravity because we have a very solid understanding of gravity. And yet, thousands of scientific books are being written every year about the nature of consciousness.

But the fact remains, the material sciences have never found the seat of consciousness, and my guess is they never will if they keep looking to some physical part of the brain or body.

We know that our brain controls where our eyes look, but we don't know how or where that choice is made. Scientists can know what we're focusing on, but not know how we are able to direct our attention. They know we focus our eyes, but not how we choose to focus our mind.

Unconsciously, we hear sounds all the time that we don't consciously register. Background noises like the sound of a refrigerator go into our brain and they go directly into our subconscious mind, but we are not consciously aware of them because we're usually focusing our attention on our thoughts.

Typically, we're either commenting on what we're seeing, which removes us from the scene, or we're worrying about the future or dwelling on the past. Most of the time we're lost in our head, unaware of what's happening around us.

If you don't believe me, pay attention to your thoughts and see how long it takes for a thought to pop into your head. If you last more than 30 seconds free from thought, you're either in the top 1% of mystics, or more likely, you're unaware that you're unaware of your thoughts.

In our modern technological society, we've lost the ability to be aware of subtlety because we've numbed our minds so much through hyperstimulating videos, entertainment, foods, drugs, and other adrenaline-pumping sports and activities.

Like an addict who's built up a tolerance, it now takes greater and greater pleasure and entertainment to jolt ourselves into the present moment. We're basically a culture of adrenaline junkies.

But this addiction has created an underlying unhappiness with our magnificent, magical, miraculous world. Today, contentment has become more rare than gold.

There is no reality, no world, no universe without consciousness. When we expand our consciousness, we expand our world. **When we become aware of our own awareness, the illusions which cause our suffering fall away effortlessly.**

This is how we break free from the duality of awareness and the content of our awareness. This is how we break free from object and subject, from witness and that which is witnessed. This is how we merge into oneness.

There is no faster way to realize oneness than through meditation. It's as simple as closing your eyes and resting in the void beyond forms. We can still hear our breath, watch our thoughts, feel our body and its sensations, and we can observe how thoughts come and go.

But we can also notice the space between thoughts. This is the birth of spaciousness, and it only continues to grow and grow.

We begin to become aware of what things we tend to think about. We notice the patterns of our thoughts and what makes thoughts pop into our head, getting to the causes of how we unconsciously shape our worldview.

We begin to understand how our mind moves from one thought to the next. We start to pay attention to how we are observing our thoughts. We focus on awareness itself, and we notice how sometimes it shines hyper focused like a laser beam, and sometimes diffused like through a lampshade.

And we become the masters of our focus, like Jimi Hendrix mastered the guitar. And a profound shift takes place as we go from the thinker of our thoughts to the awareness of thinking.

We notice how sounds and smells all constantly arise and fall away from our field of awareness. We become eternally aware of still, unchanging, eternal presence underneath the sounds and thoughts and constant change of the physical universe.

Whether we are in meditation, or we are practicing presence throughout the day, we can maintain awareness that we are aware. Eventually we stop losing sight of the fact that we are awareness perceiving. This is how we stay present and in alignment with our whole selves, our true selves.

By disidentifying with our minds and bodies, we're no longer slaves to our thoughts. We are the higher intelligence that can hear our thoughts, ignore our thoughts, believe our thoughts, or control our thoughts. Thoughts are nothing more than temporary sounds in our mind that come and go, and that have no control over us.

When we can sit in stillness and not resist the mental firestorm, we can actually find peace in it. Suddenly there's no more boredom and there's no more chasing after pleasures to fill that boredom.

There is a vast spaciousness at the deepest levels of our awareness, an emptiness onto which all our senses are projected. Like when we look closely at an atom and all we find is empty space, the deeper we look within, the more space and peace we will find.

When we're in a very quiet space and our eyes are closed, we touch this infinite space that exists within us. Sounds become faint echoes as we reside deeper and deeper in consciousness. Thoughts and emotions appear and disappear without clinging attachment, nor aversive resistance. They are no more than temporary mental projections, flashing in and out of our field of awareness, with no more importance than any other illusion.

That deep dark silence is the canvas on which all of life appears.

It is the movie screen we play our lives on. Though there is one movie screen, an infinite number of movies can play on it. It can be a comedy or a tragedy, horror or love story, true story or fantasy. The choice is up to each of us what kind of director we will be in life.

But first we have to realize that we are the directors, we are the consciousness that chooses where to point the camera, where the story goes next, how the narrator describes the events, and what characters are worth spending the most time with.

The sets will change, the costumes will change, and the plot will take some unexpected twists and turns. But that is the hallmark of any great film, and we wouldn't have it any other way. It may seem scary, but remember, it's only a movie.

A Personal Note From Todd

One last thing, my dear reader. If you have found this book even the slightest bit helpful or enjoyable, would you kindly take a minute to leave an honest review on Amazon? You have no idea how much each review helps this spiritual wisdom reach more people who are in need and struggling. Thank you from the bottom of my heart.

Much love,
Todd

ABOUT THE AUTHOR

Todd Perelmuter is a spiritual philosopher and speaker on the nature of the human mind. He has impacted the lives of millions worldwide through his teachings and his award-winning spiritual documentary films, *Aloneness to Oneness*, *You Are This Moment*, and, *The Art of Gratitude*.

Todd's goal is to make sure everyone has the tools to realize their full potential, become their most enlightened selves, and make this world a happier and more peaceful place. He shares his timeless wisdom on Youtube and on the *Path to Peace with Todd Perelmuter* podcast, helping people realize they are bigger than their thoughts, more than their past, and have limitless potential for living a life beyond their wildest dreams.

Having seen so many people around him suffering from stress, addiction, suicide, anxiety and depression, he decided to leave his comfortable life in New York City as a highly awarded writer and creative director at the world's largest ad agency. After giving away all of his belongings, he left his luxury high-rise apartment and embarked upon a 9-year journey that would take him to over 35 countries across five continents living with shamans, gurus, monks, and tribes. He studied 16 religions and spiritualities, studied with leading researchers in cognitive science, and spent 50 days meditating in a forest in total solitude, all in an effort to discover the secrets to a peaceful mind.

Todd's teachings have liberated thousands of people from their years of suffering through his work at the non-profit EastWesticism, an organization dedicated to bringing ancient wisdom and modern science from around the world to people everywhere. Go to www.EastWesticism.org to learn more and see how you can join in this important cause.

Made in United States
North Haven, CT
08 September 2024

57175935R00153